The Americans with Disabilities Act

Hiring, Accommodating and Supervising Employees with Disabilities

Mary B. Dickson

CREDITS

Editor: Kay Keppler

Layout/Design: ExecuStaff

Cover Design: Barbara Ravizza

Library of Congress 94-68538
ISBN-1-56052-311-5

The information in this book is designed to be general and timely information on the Americans with Disabilities Act of 1990 (ADA). The author is not an attorney, and she is not rendering legal advice to the reader or assistance with individual employer action. Every employment situation is different. Readers should consult the person with the disability first, then appropriate agencies or competent legal counsel regarding how these matters relate to their business or personal affairs.

ABOUT THE SERIES

The *Legal Issues for Business Series* is designed to assist managers in coping with the increasingly complex legal issues facing them in today's business environment.

In business today it is the concern for individuals and their rights that has come to our attention. Managers are not always trained in the legal implications of such concerns. The prime purpose of the series is to educate managers in areas such as sexual harassment and compliance with the Americans with Disabilities Act, so they may become more aware of these existing situations.

Each book is written by an expert in the field who is experienced in handling the many difficulties and situations managers may face.

COMPANY DESCRIPTIONS

Headquartered in California, The Employers Group is one of the nation's largest and oldest organizations dedicated exclusively to helping employers manage their human resources more effectively.

Representing nearly 5,000 employers from companies of all sizes and every line of business, The Employers Group offers information, education and consultation on many facets of personnel management.

Contact the Employers Group at 1150 South Olive Street, Suite 2300, Los Angeles, CA 90015. Phone (213) 748-0421; Facsimile (213) 742-0301.

Since it was founded in 1985, Crisp Publications has published more than 250 books and 50 videos on subjects ranging from training, management, and human resources to personal development, wellness, and adult literacy.

Crisp Publications is committed to providing organizations worldwide with the reasonably priced, quality learning materials they need to build efficient and empowered workforces.

To order Crisp books and videos or request a free catalog, contact your local distributor or Crisp Publications, Inc., 1200 Hamilton Court, Menlo Park, CA 94025. Phone: (800) 442-7477; Facsimile (415) 323-5800.

ACKNOWLEDGMENTS

A number of people contributed ideas, technical expertise and feedback during the writing and editing process. Special thanks go to:

- ❏ Gail Benson of Southern New England Telecommunications Corporation, New Haven, CT
- ❏ Carolyn Thompson of CBT Training Systems, Frankfort, IL
- ❏ Gary Jenks, Paul Short, Sue Thompson, Dan Lee and Jay Harris of SEH America, Inc., Vancouver, WA
- ❏ Ken Cross, formerly with Human Resource Specialties, Inc., Lake Oswego, OR

As a role model, Arty Trost is unsurpassed.

Kathleen Bergquist deserves special thanks for professional support and friendship, as well as commitment to full participation for people with disabilities.

Special love and thanks to Blaine Dickson for more than a quarter century of love and encouragement.

DEDICATION

This book is dedicated to

the many working people with disabilities whose skills and commitment make believers out of nonbelievers, and

employers who believe enough in themselves and in qualified people with disabilities to make a significant contribution to the workplace.

CONTENTS

PREFACE

The Americans with Disabilities Act (ADA) of 1990 has created new opportunities for America's 43 million people with disabilities. As with any new social movement or law, the ADA has also created fear and misunderstanding among people without disabilities.

As an organization, you have a choice about how you view the ADA.

❏ You can join the doomsayers who say it will result in huge lawsuits, close businesses or require extraordinary effort to employ a new group of people.

or

❏ You can look at it as an opportunity to contribute to your organization's profitability and to give qualified, talented, capable people with disabilities the dignity and financial benefits of a job that appropriately uses their skills.

and

❏ You can look at it from an economic standpoint, realizing that every time you employ a qualified person with a disability, you reduce the government expenditures that person uses. Instead, the person becomes a self-sufficient taxpayer who contributes to the economic growth of your community and the country.

The goal of this book is to help you understand the ADA and its implications for employment practices within your organization.

# INTRODUCTION

> ## What Would You Do?
>
> Dan Lee, a man in his early 20s, has worked for SEH America in Vancouver, Washington, for several years mounting extremely thin, diamond-edged internal diameter saw blades. It is a fast-paced job, with a significant loss of production if he couldn't keep up the pace. Each blade costs $400, and if not mounted properly, the product is ruined, or at least causes extensive rework. If the blades are not tensioned to exacting standards, it causes an extreme safety hazard. Specifications require blades to be adjusted to ±25 microns (1/1000 inch). Making adjustments of this degree of accuracy requires extremely good manual and fine finger dexterity.
>
> In 1992, Dan Lee lost his right (dominant) arm in a water skiing accident. Today, he is back on the job, at full production, using a prosthetic arm.
>
> Ask yourself, "If I were the manager, would I think that someone with the use of only his nondominant arm and hand could perform a job requiring such dexterity? Would I want to take a chance on an employee like this? How could he do the job? What would I have to do to accommodate him?"

Many people would answer these questions with negatives. We grew up with cultural programming that told us not to expect people with disabilities to work alongside us in industry. We have a hard time imagining how such a person could be productive and meet exacting quality standards.

With the Americans with Disabilities Act (ADA) now changing the way we do business, we need to put aside our cultural programming and accept and include qualified people with disabilities in our workplace, tapping them for the contribution they can make to our organization's mission. The Americans with Disabilities Act of 1990 offers organizations opportunities to include qualified people with disabilities in their workforce in new and exciting ways.

This book will help you recognize that:

❏ The ADA is a manageable law, although it may require making some changes in the way you run your business

❏ You can implement the ADA while maintaining productivity and harmonious working relationships

❏ You can communicate effectively with people regardless of physical or mental disabilities

❏ Nondisabled colleagues of people with disabilities can accept and get along with disabled coworkers while maintaining confidentiality about physical and mental conditions

People become disabled for many reasons. Some, like Dan Lee, are involved in accidents. Some workers, long valued for their contributions to a company's bottom line, face the potential of a disabling condition, from repetitive motion syndrome, cancer, loss of vision or hearing. How would you treat your employees should they become disabled? Will their disability make any difference in their productivity or the way you and their coworkers relate to them?

Your organization's attitude is a key factor. Communication skills, willingness to cope with change, and creativity are all skills that will make you successful in implementing the ADA.

Hiring People with Disabilities

As an organization, you hire people who can help you make money or provide good service. You have undoubtedly noticed that the workplace is changing, and you have a different pool of applicants than you have had in the past.

That pool now includes qualified people with disabilities. Although many people think that the ADA is responsible for introducing this new element of the workforce, many companies discovered long before the ADA that disabled employees were productive workers. Results are consistent among all studies from 1948 to 1990.

- ❑ Work performance: good to excellent

- ❑ Insurance costs: no increase

- ❑ Turnover: lower than workers without disabilities

- ❑ Absenteeism: lower than coworkers without disabilities

- ❑ Accident rates: lower than other employees

- ❑ Accommodations: perceived by companies as not prohibitively costly

The survey highlights of a 1991 Harris Poll reveal that "more than four out of five Americans believe that disabled workers are equally or more productive than average workers. However, only just over half of those with a regular job rate their employers' policies for the employment of disabled people positively."

Some people worry about how coworkers would feel about having their work hours or job duties changed to accommodate a coworker with a disability. A study done by the Bureau of National Affairs in early 1992 found that more than half would think it was fair, another quarter might not think it was fair but would not protest, and only 16% would protest. That number will probably decrease as people have positive experiences with disabled colleagues.

Many companies have hired disabled workers with great success.

- ❑ Marriott Corporation has hired more than 8,000 people with disabilities and has found a lower turnover rate than among their nondisabled employees.

- Pizza Hut has calculated that it has saved more than $2.2 million in turnover costs.

- Little Tikes Company, of Hudson, Ohio, hired 15 hearing impaired workers and provided accommodations such as flashing lights on forklifts, an interpreter for the monthly staff meeting and sign language classes for hearing employees. They also created transitional jobs to return injured workers to work. They have realized a high retention rate and impressive levels of dedication and commitment to the company.

- The University of Massachusetts Medical Center has hired nearly 400 employees and one assistant with disabilities. Accommodations cost less than $700 annually.

- SEH America, Inc., in Vancouver, Washington, has a successful supported employment program that employs workers with developmental disabilities.

It is not only large, well-known companies that have found capable employees with disabilities making a difference. Companies of all sizes, in small towns and large cities, benefit from hiring good employees.

- John Zandy, a partner in a Connecticut law firm, says of employing an intern with a disability, "I gave him difficult assignments, and he returned high-quality legal work. We simply gave someone with a good mind an opportunity to excel."

- Kreonite, Inc., manufacturer of photographic and graphic arts film based in Wichita, Kansas, has dropped its turnover rate from 32% to 10%–12% by hiring persons with disabilities.

Many people also change their attitudes when they work with qualified people with disabilities. One supervisor said, "As a result of our experience with a developmentally disabled employee, the 40 people in this department no longer frown on things like Special Olympics. Their fears of people with disabilities are gone. They are more warm-hearted and look at people with disabilities face to face. This experience has changed us all forever."

Companies Benefit from Expanded Customer Base

Other organizations are recognizing the potential increase in customers that the ADA represents and take steps to meet their needs. As a Sears official said, "43 million people with disabilities equals 43 million potential customers."

Example: Barrier-free Business Opens its Doors to Customers with Disabilities

The desire to open his business to a new group of customers motivated a call to the Job Accommodation Network (JAN) by the owner of a hardware and swimming pool supply store. The businessowner wanted to make the store accessible for persons with various disabilities. A JAN consultant discussed modification options, including ramping the entrance way, installing automatic door systems, installing telephone devices for the deaf and other possibilities.[1]

Example: Accommodation Opens Job to Candidate Who Is Disabled and Creates New Service/Market for Company

When a bank bought some equipment that allowed a person who is deaf to work as a teller, the bank also gained the ability to serve customers who are deaf. Interested in hiring a candidate who was deaf, the bank manager called JAN for assistance. Because the position required conversations with hearing customers, JAN suggested that teller and customer could communicate using telecommunication devices for the deaf (TDDs). Though TDDs are most often used on phone lines, JAN knew of another device to connect two units without using a phone line. With the TDDs, a customer and the teller could communicate by typing on the TDD keyboard.[2]

Match Game Exercise

Match up the following well-known people in column 1 and their disability in column 2. Then think about the contribution each has made to society.

CONTRIBUTOR	DISABILITY
Cher	Head injury
Chris Burke	Polio
Bruce Jenner	Blind
James Brady	Learning disability
Stephen Hawking	Orthopedic impairment
Ray Charles	Polio
Ann Jillian	Visual impairment
Whoopi Goldberg	Epilepsy
Senator Robert Dole	Learning disability
Itzhak Perlman	Mental illness
Marlee Matlin	Dyslexia
President John F. Kennedy	Multiple sclerosis
Mary Tyler Moore	Deaf
Danny Glover	Down's syndrome
Sammy Davis, Jr.	Back problems
Annette Funicello	Amyotrophic lateral sclerosis
Governor George Wallace	Diabetes
President Franklin Roosevelt	Multiple sclerosis
Margaux Hemingway	Epilepsy
Virginia Woolf	Cancer
Representative Barbara Jordan	Paraplegia

Compare your answers with those listed in Appendix B on page 127.

Someone in your organization has probably already joined this list of stars. Who in your company has made a contribution while living and working with a disability? _____

_____

Not all people with disabilities are famous. Thousands live productive lives without ever being in the spotlight. However, you can see from this list that people with disabilities can achieve greatness. If you see someone who uses a wheelchair and wonder how that person could possibly do the job, just remember the president who served this country longer than any other holder of that office.

Developing a Business Philosophy about the ADA

Every organization has a "culture" that defines the way it treats its employees and customers. You will want to develop a philosophy of how you will comply with the ADA and treat qualified people with disabilities.

Let's look at three possible ADA philosophies. Consider where you fit now, then monitor your attitude as you work through this book.

Traditional. Traditional organizations may:

❏ Regard the ADA as just another law and will do the minimum necessary to ensure compliance

❏ Never have had any contact with people with disabilities and think that they should stay home or in an institution or work in sheltered workshops, if at all

❏ Be concerned that hiring a person with a disability would cause problems with coworker acceptance, lowered productivity and poor quality

Hesitant. The hesitant organization may:

❏ Be aware of the ADA and its general provisions, but not worry about the details

❏ Think people with disabilities who work are "amazing" and "courageous," but cannot imagine having someone with a disability working for them

❏ Hire a person with a disability hesitantly, and if that person did not work out, would not hire another one

Progressive. As a progressive, this organization may:

❏ Look at new initiatives, laws and regulations as somewhat of a bother to learn about, but once it understands them, it will wholeheartedly comply

❏ Aggressively seek ways in which the laws can benefit the organization

- ❏ Have hired qualified people with disabilities in the past and feel comfortable interacting with them

- ❏ Look at the ADA and ask how this can help meet organizational goals or establish organizational leadership in this area

- ❏ Look for opportunities to establish links with schools and organizations that help find employment for qualified people with disabilities and offer employment to someone with potential

Individuals in progressive organizations realize that they may take this opportunity to challenge their own beliefs about disability in the same way they challenge their racist, sexist, ageist, homophobic and other biased beliefs.

Where do you and your organization fit in this list of characteristics? Are you closer to a traditional than a progressive, or do you fit someplace in the middle? Keep in mind that how you handle change in general may affect the way you cope with the ADA.

Here's an example of progressive thinking and resulting actions.

Example

Emmy-winning actress Suzanne Rogers is the beautiful Maggie Horton to millions of NBC-TV *Days of Our Lives* viewers. Eleven years into playing the soap opera character, Rogers awoke one morning unable to speak, smile or swallow—one side of her face was paralyzed. Diagnosed with myasthenia gravis, a chronic muscle disease that produced weakness and abnormally rapid fatigue, Rogers's thymus gland was removed. As a result of medication, the star's face became bloated and her luxuriant red hair thinned.

What job accommodation did the show's producers provide? A makeup artist? A hairdresser? Certainly, but the real job accommodation Rogers received was a story line in scripts that incorporated her illness into Maggie Horton's character. Her fictional portrayal mirrored her own day-to-day battles—voice weakness, eye drooping, hospitalization. As Rogers's condition improved, so did Horton's.

Days of Our Lives producers made an appropriate and reasonable accommodation in a unique situation. Rogers's experience illustrates that all job accommodations are not prewritten in a master guidebook somewhere, but may be the result of the creative efforts of the employer and the individual with the disability.

Before you begin to work through this book, take this true/false quiz, which tests your understanding of the Americans with Disabilities Act. (See Appendix B, page 128, for the answers.)

True or False Quiz

The ADA is designed to remove employment barriers for qualified individuals with disabilities. The ADA requires employers to identify what reasonable accommodations might be necessary to allow an employee to perform the essential functions of a specific job. The following quiz will help determine the training needs of your organization to address full and equal employment opportunities for all individuals under this law. Circle the correct answer.

True	False	
T	F	1. The Americans with Disabilities Act protects all qualified individuals with disabilities regardless of their citizenship status or nationality.
T	F	2. An individual with a disability may choose to file a legal claim under a state discrimination law.
T	F	3. When symptoms of a disability are controlled by medication, an individual is no longer considered disabled.
T	F	4. Individuals who were economically disadvantaged as children qualify as disabled.
T	F	5. Obesity is not generally considered a disabling impairment.
T	F	6. The presence of a physical impairment is sufficient evidence of a disability.
T	F	7. Acceptance of an individual with a disability by coworkers or customers is important to the hiring process.
T	F	8. An employer may consider the applicant's future health when making an employment decision.
T	F	9. The essential function of a job may be directly related to the size of the staff.

T   F   **10.** Job descriptions are required by the Americans with Disabilities Act.

T   F   **11.** A job applicant with chronic breathing problems requiring frequent rest periods that affect productivity would be protected by the ADA.

T   F   **12.** Employers must modify the job application process to enable equal opportunities to qualified applicants with disabilities.

T   F   **13.** Employers may offer a health insurance policy that excludes coverage for pre-existing conditions.

T   F   **14.** An employee unable to perform a job with a reasonable accommodation must be considered for reassignment to another available position.

T   F   **15.** Employees may be required to eat lunch at their desks if the company cafeteria is inaccessible.

T   F   **16.** If accessible public transportation delays the arrival of an employee by 15 minutes, this chronic tardiness is grounds for dismissal.

T   F   **17.** Cost may be a reason for not making an accommodation.

T   F   **18.** Employers may exclude a job applicant who poses a direct risk to the safety of others.

T   F   **19.** Testing for illegal use of drugs is prohibited by the Americans with Disabilities Act.

T   F   **20.** A nondisabled job applicant who shares a home with an AIDS patient is not a good candidate because of the possibility of frequent absences.

T   F   **21.** When several effective accommodations are available, the employer must comply with the employee's preference.

T   F   **22.** Employers may be found liable for not addressing reasonable accommodations for an employee who has kept secret a disability.

T	F	**23.** When a reasonable accommodation allows someone with a disability to perform a job, that applicant must be given preference over other candidates.
T	F	**24.** If a necessary accommodation is refused, the employee may no longer be considered qualified.
T	F	**25.** When it is obvious that a job applicant is disabled (example: uses a wheelchair), ADA encourages inquiries about the nature of the disability.
T	F	**26.** Dexterity tests may be given at any time during the job application process.
T	F	**27.** A job offer may be contingent on the results of a medical examination.
T	F	**28.** Medical information should be routinely updated and kept in the employee's personnel file.
T	F	**29.** An employee could pay for providing a reasonable accommodation if it was found to be an undue hardship for the employer.
T	F	**30.** The Americans with Disabilities Act encourages alternative solutions to resolve disputes before legal action.

See Appendix B on page 127 for the answers to the quiz.

P A R T
one

The Americans with Disabilities Act of 1990

The Americans with Disabilities Act was signed into law by President George Bush on July 26, 1990. Its purpose is to provide equal opportunities in all aspects of life for America's 43 million people with disabilities.

The ADA's five sections, called Titles, cover the following.

Title I: Employment
Title II: Public Services
Title III: Public Accommodations
Title IV: Telecommunications
Title V: Miscellaneous

This book concentrates on Title I. Realize that if you work in a government organization, covered by Title II, you are also covered by Titles I and III, as well as other laws that prohibit discrimination against persons with disabilities, such as portions of the Rehabilitation Act of 1973, as amended.

History of the ADA

The ADA is one of a long line of laws designed to bring people with disabilities into the mainstream of American life.

❏ The Civil Rights Act of 1964 forbids discrimination based on race, religion, ethnicity and sex. Originally, it did not include people with disabilities.

❏ The Rehabilitation Act of 1973 forbids federal contractors from discriminating against people with disabilities and requires job accommodations for those who need them.

❏ Other laws have affected transportation and housing for people with disabilities. No law provided all the rights and privileges of citizenship to America's disabled citizens. The ADA is meant to rectify that oversight.

There is an important distinction between the ADA, which is a "nondiscrimination" law and other laws that require "affirmative action."

❏ "Nondiscrimination" means equal opportunity to apply for and work in jobs and be considered for promotion along with other qualified people

❏ "Affirmative action" means that an organization plans for and actively seeks candidates in protected classes

The ADA has no recruiting requirements. It does require that organizations look first at a person's *a*bilities rather than automatically excluding them on the basis of perceived *in*ability resulting from a *dis*ability.

Who Is Covered by the ADA?

Title I of the ADA, which prohibits discrimination in hiring, took effect for companies with 25 or more employees on July 26, 1992 and for companies of 15 or more employees on July 26, 1994. It covers all employers, including state and federal agencies, except private membership clubs. Title I of the ADA impacts all aspects of employment.

The ADA is a comprehensive law. If your organization is large enough, then all employees are covered.

❏ CEO to the janitor (all job titles)

❏ Employees who already have a disability

❏ Employees who become disabled in the future

❏ Applicants and newly hired employees

❏ Those who associate with people with disabilities

Disabled Employees

Your organization may already have disabled employees. Some of the disabilities may be visible, such as someone who has a mobility impairment and uses a wheelchair or crutches to get around. You may have someone who is legally blind or is deaf, or someone with severe arthritis.

Consider, in addition, that you may have employees who are disabled but whose disabilities have never been recognized. For example, 10%–15% of the working population is considered learning disabled. Someone who is an excellent assembly worker may have difficulty filling out a work order or completing statistical process control paperwork. The individual may have a learning disability that affects the ability to complete paperwork accurately.

Someone may hide a visual loss for fear of dismissal should it become known. You may have someone who is HIV positive but has not told anyone in the organization for fear of being fired. You may have someone who has cancer but has not let anyone know.

Since the ADA, more people with disabilities are becoming aware of their rights and employees may now have the courage to come to you and request accommodation. You need to be prepared for this possibility.

Employees Who Become Disabled

Disability is only a heartbeat or footstep away for any of us. Recognizing that, the ADA protects from discrimination any employee who may become disabled, either on the job or off.

Applicants and Newly Hired Employees

The ADA will encourage more people with disabilities to enter the workforce for the first time, including:

❑ People who have been disabled all of their lives, but have never before worked

- ❏ Those who have been employed as disabled workers, but for a different organization

- ❏ Young people with disabilities who have been provided services under Public Law 94-142 and the Individuals with Disabilities Education Act

These young people may be different from others because their disabilities have been accommodated in the school setting, perhaps all of their educational life. They will expect accommodation as they move into the workforce. They will be more knowledgeable about their rights as disabled Americans than older workers who become disabled.

Associates of People with Disabilities

The ADA recognizes that discrimination exists against people who live with or associate with people with disabilities. A mother who has a son with cerebral palsy, for example, may be perceived by her employer as someone who may need extensive time off to care for him. Someone who volunteers in a hospice may be perceived as a person at risk for becoming disabled. While the ADA does not require employers to accommodate those who associate with people with disabilities, it does require that we not discriminate against them in any aspect of employment.

Who Is Disabled under the ADA?

The following format is explanatory material, relating directly to the law, about each topic taken from the same source. Called "The ADA Says," this section will provide the reader with a fast and easy way to identify material taken directly from the ADA, such as definitions.

> ### The ADA Says...
>
> An "individual with a disability" is someone who has a *physical or mental impairment* that *substantially limits* one or more *major life activities*, has a *record of such an impairment* or is *regarded as having such an impairment.*[1]
>
> Persons who have a known association or relationship with an individual with a disability are also protected from discrimination.

ADA Key Phrases

Let's take a closer look at the key phrases in this definition.

> ### The ADA Says...
>
> "Physical impairment" is defined as "any physiological disorder, or condition, cosmetic disfigurement or anatomical loss affecting one or more of the following body systems: neurological, musculoskeletal, special sense organs, respiratory (including speech organs), cardiovascular, reproductive, digestive, genitourinary, hemic and lymphatic, skin and endocrine."
>
> "Mental impairment" is defined as "any mental or psychological disorder, such as mental retardation, organic brain syndrome, emotional or mental illness and specific learning disabilities."[2]

There is no comprehensive list of all impairments, since they can occur singly or in combination. An impairment is determined without regard to medications or assistive devices that a person may use. For example, a person may use an artificial leg but may still be considered disabled. Contagious diseases are considered impairments, although an employer does not have to hire or retain anyone whose contagious disease poses a direct threat to health or safety if no reasonable accommodation could reduce or eliminate the threat.

The ADA Says...

"Substantially limits" means that "an individual must be unable to perform, or be significantly limited in the ability to perform, an activity compared to an average person in the general population." It is not only the impairment that is important, but how it affects an individual's ability to perform life activities. Three factors are considered in determining whether an impairment substantially limits major life activities: nature and severity, how long it will last or is expected to last and permanent or long-term impact or expected impact.[3]

This means that certain events may not qualify a person for protection under the ADA. For example, pregnancy is not considered a disability because it is not a long-term condition.

The ADA Says...

"Major life activities" are "activities that an average person can perform with little or no difficulty," such as walking, talking, breathing, seeing, hearing, learning, working, caring for oneself, lifting, standing or performing manual tasks.[4]

Sometimes an individual will have more than one impairment, and it is the combination that makes a person "disabled" under the ADA.

This is important when reviewing school records, which may indicate that a person was in a class for people with mental retardation, when, in fact, the person was misdiagnosed and had a specific learning disability.

This part of the definition recognizes that an individual may have an impairment that is not substantially limiting, but is treated by an employer as being significant. An individual may have an impairment that is limiting only because of the attitudes of others or someone may not have an impairment but is regarded as having an impairment.

This is crucial to understand, since you, as a potential employer, can make people disabled when they are not. If you refuse to hire someone for a front-desk receptionist job because the person has facial scars resulting from burns or a birthmark and cannot show a legitimate, nondiscriminatory reason for your action, you may be in trouble under the ADA.

Even if you don't want to hire someone with a scarred face, the ADA asks us to accept all people into the mainstream of our society. That means learning to accept people who do not fit the Hollywood definition of attractive. Very few jobs other than professional model require a person to be attractive to perform the essential functions of the position successfully.

The longer the ADA has been in effect, the more types of disabilities appear to be covered. In some cases, obesity or nicotine addiction may cause a person to be considered disabled. Before assuming a person is not covered, check with your HR department or a knowledgeable attorney.

Can you think of anyone in your organization who meets any of the above criteria of disabilities? _____

_____

You cannot base an adverse employment decision on unsubstantiated concerns about productivity, safety, insurance, liability, attendance, costs of accommodation, accessibility, workers' compensation costs or acceptance by coworkers and customers. This may be one of the most difficult concepts under the ADA to accept, but the ADA requires that you make employment decisions based only on a person's skills and abilities.

Exclusions

A person who currently illegally uses drugs is not protected under the ADA. It would be prudent to discuss the latest information on drug and alcohol use and the ADA with an attorney if you need to take any actions regarding a specific applicant or employee.

Physical characteristics such as eye or hair color are not included under ADA protection. Neither are temporary conditions such as broken limbs, colds, flu and pregnancy unless complications cause more severe conditions. Personality traits such as a quick temper are not ADA-protected. Environmental, cultural or economic disadvantages are not considered to be impairments.

Homosexuality and bisexuality are not considered to be impairments and are therefore not disabilities covered by the ADA.

> ### *The ADA Says...*
>
> "Disability does not include transvestism, transsexualism, pedophilia, exhibitionism, voyeurism, gender identity disorders not resulting from physical impairments, or other sexual behavior disorders; compulsive gambling, kleptomania, pyromania; or psychoactive substance use disorders resulting from current illegal use of drugs."

The Impact of Disabilities

How many people are affected by these regulations? The U.S. Census Bureau defines "work disability" as "a health problem or disability that prevents you from working or limits the amount or kind of work you can do."

The March 1991 *Current Population Survey* estimates that 14,648,000 Americans aged 16–64 have a work disability. Of those, 29% are employed full- or parttime, while 71% are unemployed.

The National Center for Health Statistics estimates the prevalence of various types of impairments in the U.S. population of all ages.

Note that most of these disabilities are invisible, so be careful not to assume that you don't already have people with disabilities in your workforce.

Impairment	Number per 1,000 people
Hearing impairment	94.7
Visual impairment	30.6
Speech impairment	9.3
Arthritis	125.3
Epilepsy	4.8
Missing extremities (excluding toes and fingers)	5.0
Partial/complete paralysis	5.9
Diabetes	25.3
Hypertension	110.2
Heart disease	78.5
Kidney trouble	12.4
Back injury	70.3

(Reported in *In the Mainstream,* November/December 1992, p. 18.)

Other figures from other sources:

❏ Persons with mental retardation = 1%–2% of noninstitutionalized population

❏ Cerebral palsy = two of every 1,000 people

❏ Wheelchair users = 1.4 million people

❏ Learning disabilities = 12–25 million people

❏ Severe long-term mental illness = 2.5 million people

❏ Arthritis is the leading cause of functional limitations in the United States, affecting 78 of every 1,000 people in the prime working years between ages 45 and 54, and 125 of every 1,000 people of all ages.

- Heart disease hits seven million Americans, 280,000 of whom have bypass surgery by age 45 and then return to work (often much healthier after surgery than they were before).

- AIDS affects many working-age Americans; one of every four patients is 40–49 years old.

- Chronic low back pain is most prevalent between ages 45 and 64 and, in some professions, is the leading cause of disability.

- Vision decreases after age 40, with several age-related conditions occurring around age 55.

This should give you some idea of the numbers of people who may benefit from the ADA. Keep in mind that "disabled people come in groups of one, and you can't make generalizations," according to one of the authors of the ADA, Chris Bell.

Physical Disabilities

When we think of the word "disabled," we may picture someone using a wheelchair or a dog guide. We think of a visible physical disability or someone with Down's Syndrome or mental retardation, since it often has physical manifestations. Other disabilities such as epilepsy are invisible.

Epilepsy deserves specific mention, since a lack of information contributes to unintentional discrimination against many of the two million Americans with the condition. Employers are concerned that an employee with epilepsy may have a seizure on the job. According to Frierson, ". . . most epileptic employees will never have a . . . seizure at work. At least 80% of all people with epilepsy have the condition completely under control by the use of medication. Many of the 20% who occasionally have seizures will tend to have them at night, and even if they occur at work, most seizures are quite mild." All states now issue driver's licenses to people with epilepsy if they are seizure free.

Epilepsy is the single largest category of impairment leading to lawsuits under the 1973 Rehabilitation Act and similar state laws. If you know that an applicant or employee has epilepsy, learn more about the condition so you can avoid discriminatory employment actions.

If you know an applicant or employee has *any* condition with which you are unfamiliar, learn about it before assuming anything about the person's inabilities to do a job.

Mental and Emotional Disabilities

Mental retardation, mental illness, learning disabilities and traumatic brain injury are often more misunderstood than physical impairments. From early days, we are afraid of people who are labeled "crazy," "retarded" or "dumb." Until we get to know someone with such a disability, we assume the worst about their capabilities and behaviors. We may fail to consider hiring a person with such a disability because of concerns about productivity, safety, insurance, liability, attendance and acceptance by coworkers and customers.

Developmental Disabilities (Mental Retardation)

Developmental disabilities affect people differently than mental illnesses. Developmental disabilities include Down's syndrome, which results in mental retardation. This simply means that someone learns more slowly than the average. The individual may also lack social skills. However, many employers have found that people with developmental disabilities can be productive workers in jobs that suit their skills.

As one supervisor of a developmentally disabled person said, "The worst obstacle was fear. Once the fear dissipated, it was easier, and it will be easier for us the next time we hire someone with a disability."

Mental Illness

Mental disorders, including schizophrenia, depression, bipolar disorder, panic disorders and obsessive-compulsive disorders, affect about one in five adults.

Members of your work force may have an emotional or mental disorder but may choose not to tell you about it because they may feel you will treat them differently, not consider them for promotion or will tell coworkers. All of these actions limit the worker's potential and are discriminatory under the ADA.

More is being learned all the time about disorders such as schizophrenia, once considered a "split personality." Now it is understood as a disturbance of the processing of information, during which a person's thoughts may be fragmented, or the ability to integrate information properly may be impaired. A person with a psychiatric disability may need accommodation to handle such issues as:

❏ Concentrating

❏ Screening out environmental stimuli

❏ Maintaining stamina through the workday

❏ Managing time pressures and deadlines

❏ Initiating interpersonal contact

❏ Focusing on multiple tasks simultaneously

❏ Responding to negative feedback

❏ Coping with the physical and emotional side effects of medications

For a person with a mental disorder to succeed on the job, employers need to maintain a positive attitude about the person's employability, accurately define essential job functions, provide appropriate accommodations and make sure the employee has full access to all privileges of employment. Note that these are essential characteristics in assuring success of any employee.

Learning Disabilities

Learning disabilities are different than mental retardation. It is estimated that 10%–15% of the working population has some form of a learning disability, affecting job performance in learning, reading, writing, spelling and computation skills, as well as others. Many adults with learning disabilities do not know that they have that diagnosis, they just know that they have a hard time completing paperwork or spelling accurately. Others have been diagnosed and may have learned coping strategies so they can complete all aspects of their work accurately.

Chronic and Progressive Conditions

It is tempting to assume that once a person is disabled, the disability is static and any accommodations will be made at the beginning of employment. However, many disabilities, including arthritis, AIDS, diabetes, some types of vision loss, amyotrophic lateral sclerosis, cancer and others, change over time.

Someone who has a past history of cancer may be cured, but is still protected under the ADA under the second part of the definition of a "qualified individual with a disability" because discrimination remains. People who return to work after cancer treatments report being denied employment, promotion and fringe benefits; transferred to different jobs or demoted; refused accommodation or even terminated.

Do you have a friend or family member who had an illness and then had difficulty re-entering the workforce? What obstacles did he or she have to overcome? _____

_____

No other aspect of employment is as difficult as watching a formerly productive employee cope with a progressively worsening physical condition. Some conditions do not improve, but worsen over time.

You need to accommodate the person in any way you can, but you also need to be prepared when he or she is no longer able to do the job and no accommodation will work. Supervisors should base discussions strictly on the essential functions of the job, asking the employee whether he or she can do those functions, with or without accommodation. Most people will recognize when they can no longer function effectively.

You may need to get support for other staff as well as the employee. Within the limitations of confidentiality, encourage the employee to involve company medical officials or the employee's own medical provider, others who are knowledgeable about the person and his or her disability for support and accurate information. Have someone "on call" in case other employees request information or assistance. Offer your Employee Assistance Program for support for the employee, co-workers, and supervisors.

Fitness for Duty

> ### The ADA Says...
>
> "Fitness for duty" is another qualification standard to consider. The ADA defines fitness for duty as "the degree of risk justifying disqualification that demonstrates reasonable probability of serious or substantial harm."

Employment decisions made on this basis must also be based on information from objective data about known risk factors and possible accommodations.

If you make an employment decision based on either direct threat or fitness for duty, you will want to check it with your human resource department or attorney. Remember, the greatest number of lawsuits filed under Title I of the ADA during 1992 were for wrongful discharge.

■ ■

**Disability
Education
Exercise**

I am familiar with the following disabilities and their effects on the workplace. _____

_____

_____

I need to learn about these disabilities: _____

_____

_____

Sources available for me to learn include: _____

_____

_____

I will make these learning opportunities available to employees:

_____

■ ■

PART TWO

Updating Our Attitudes and Abilities about People with Disabilities

Stereotypes we learned as children could affect our ability to implement ADA adequately now in the workforce

The success of ADA implementation depends on management support and philosophy

Training for all employees in ADA compliance should include legal aspects and sensitivity training

Organizations have choices about the way they implement and comply with the ADA. The choices an organization makes will be based on the attitudes and perceptions of decision makers at all levels.

Saying the word "disabled" is enough to throw many people into a complex series of emotional responses. Let's review where these emotions, and their resulting attitudes, came from.

The Origin of Attitudes

People with disabilities traditionally have been viewed as "special," "different," even "exotic." For example:

Many parents said to their children, "Don't stare at people with disabilities; it's not polite." Our natural curiosity and potential acceptance of people with disabilities was discouraged. We were probably not encouraged to make friends with disabled class-mates or invite them to lunch or to our house. This may have been similar to what we learned about people whose skin color or religion were different from ours.

Movies we saw long ago showed people with disabilities as objects of pity, like Tiny Tim in *A Christmas Carol,* or as special or super-human beings, like Helen Keller. Today's TV shows offer a chance to see competent people with disabilities working and interacting quite differently; for example, Benny in *L.A. Law* and Corky in *Life Goes On,* are men with developmental disabilities and Tess, is an attorney who is deaf, in *Reasonable Doubts.*

Our schools once put children with disabilities in special education classes, depriving us as youngsters of opportunities to interact with people with disabilities. Now, children with disabilities are mainstreamed as much as possible. In addition, we are starting to see teachers with disabilities in our schools.

Example

Robbie Thomas, who uses a wheelchair for mobility, teaches physical education at Parkridge Elementary School and coaches varsity soccer at Stafford Senior High School in Stafford, Virginia. Isn't being a wheelchair user a disadvantage for a PE teacher? Not for Thomas. He's always in the heat of the action, playing sports alongside his students. Thomas thinks of his wheelchair as an advantage because it allows him to see eye-to-eye with his young charges, creating a greater intimacy than if he were standing.[1]

Consider the message that this will send to Robbie's students as they are forming their attitudes about people with disabilities.

We were told to be good or we would end up like people with disabilities. We were made to feel afraid of anyone who was different. Today, we are more likely to recognize that people with disabilities are not evil or being punished for something they have done.

We learned to equate disability with sickness. These days, we watch wheelchair athletes and participants in Special Olympics use their bodies to achieve athletic feats.

We learned that we should be nice to people with disabilities, to feel sorry for them, and not to expect much from them. This attitude may not have changed much!

We may carry around the myths and stereotypes we learned from the way our culture taught us. Society is now changing; however, and we need to revise our thinking!

As a result of what we learned early in life, we may not expect people with disabilities to be productive workers or lead happy lives!

First Contact with a Person with a Disability

Check below those people with disabilities with whom you have had personal contact at various stages in your life. Put a ✔ in the square indicating the first person with a disability you remember.

Name of Person _____

When	Parent	Sibling	Spouse	Family	Neighbor	Stranger
Preschool						
Grade School						
High School						
College						
Work						

After you have completed this chart, notice at what point in your life most of your contacts came. Were you very young, or was your first experience later in life?

Initial Impressions of People with Disabilities

Let's look a little more in depth at the effect these people had on your life.

1. When my parents or teachers told me about people with disabilities, they said:

    _____

    _____

    _____

2. The first person with a disability I knew was:

    _____

3. When I was near the person, I felt:

_____

_____

_____

4. When I was in school, I had the following experiences with classmates or a teacher with disabilities:

_____

_____

_____

5. Since I've been in the workplace, my experiences with people with disabilities have been:

_____

_____

_____

Possible Life Experiences

We may have had family members or friends with disabilities. Their experiences (and ours) depended on our family situation, economics, religion and other factors.

- ❑ Our mother lost her vision because of diabetes and had to give up her profession

- ❑ Our sister with developmental disabilities was raised in a state institution and works in a sheltered workshop

- ❑ Our grandfather, who had polio as a child, had doors slammed in his face because during his working years, people who limped were excluded from the workforce

How might your life experiences influence you in your workplace? Consider the decisions you might make, policies you might create and communication you might have: _____

_____

_____

Our experiences may have been more positive.

- ❏ Our mother, who was blind, continued her career successfully with the help of specialized equipment

- ❏ Our sister, who is developmentally disabled, may be working and living on her own

- ❏ Our grandfather may have been a successful advertising executive.

How might these experiences influence you in your workplace? Consider again the decisions you might make, policies you might create and communication you might have with people:

_____

_____

_____

We may be open to hiring qualified individuals with disabilities because of these early, positive experiences.

There's another possibility. You may know or have known a person with a disability who was exceptional in some way. Perhaps a blind friend was a wonderful musician, or a person who used a wheelchair was an outstanding athlete. Maybe you saw TV coverage of the young man who uses one artificial leg and completed the Bicycle Race Across America.

Do not generalize from these experiences that all people with disabilities are musical or athletic or have some other "super" powers. These become the new stereotypes and myths that may give us unrealistically high expectations. The old myths and stereotypes limit people with disabilities; the new myths and stereotypes may set people up to be more than human. We need to accept people with disabilities as people, with the entire range of abilities and disabilities that humanness includes.

The attitudes you bring to work may mean that you struggle with the idea of having qualified people with disabilities at your job. Negative attitudes conflict with what we must do under the ADA. The law says we must consider people with disabilities as competent, productive members of the workforce. We may need to make reasonable accommodations, but we do not have to accept lower quality or quantity from employees who have disabilities.

Organizational

Some of us struggle with the requirements of the ADA and the idea of having qualified people with disabilities in our workplace. We don't expect to see people with disabilities working, so we might be hesitant to hire them; if they are there, we would not expect high quality work from them. If, by some chance, they appeared in our organization, we would be nice to them, take care of them and think they are wonderful and courageous to even try to work.

> *These may seem like mixed messages, and they are until we resolve them!*

HR Department

The human resources department must bring a positive attitude to organizational policies. This department needs to be especially careful to formulate decisions and positions that are fully in accordance with the ADA and create an atmosphere of acceptance and inclusion.

Supervisors' Attitudes

Supervisors may have some of the following concerns about a person with a disability reporting to them. Check any you have seen in your organization.

- ❏ People with disabilities don't really want to work.

- ❏ It's hard to talk to a person with a disability.

- ❏ The staff would not want to work with a person with a disability.

- ❏ It's more difficult (or impossible) to supervise someone with a disability.

❏ The department budget cannot afford reasonable accommodations for an employee with a disability.

❏ If an employee with a disability did not work out, it would be impossible to fire the person.

Other concerns that supervisors might express in your organization:

_____

_____

_____

Stop! Do not go on until you've thought about this and answered the following question!

Three things I've learned from this exercise about my attitudes are:

1. _____

2. _____

3. _____

Recognize your own reaction to people with disabilities by reviewing your answers to the earlier quizzes. Admit your own reactions. If they are negative, find a way to update them.

To gain information:

❏ Contact local agencies that train and place people with disabilities in jobs

❏ Talk with other employers who have successfully hired employees with disabilities

❏ Find supervisors in your own organization who have supervised employees with disabilities

❏ Talk with disabled people about their employment experiences

❏ Expose yourself to people who have had positive experiences

❏ Look for and celebrate successful experiences with disabled people, both in your personal life and on the job

What else can you do to update your attitudes towards people with disabilities?

_____

_____

_____

Employees' Attitudes

You can help the employees in your organization improve their attitudes by being a role model. Take steps such as these to reduce misperceptions, myths and stereotypes.

❑ Talk with employees, either individually or in small, informal groups, to understand their perceptions. Maybe they have no qualms about having coworkers with disabilities. Perhaps they have had positive personal or professional experiences that have led them to accept people with disabilities.

❑ Introduce qualified people with disabilities as another aspect of diversifying the workplace. If your organization offers training on diversity, ensure that disability issues are covered in the training. Request that such training cover laws as well as awareness, sensitivity and communication skills. This will help employees feel more comfortable in working with people who are different from those with whom they are accustomed to working.

❑ Include a video on disability awareness and sensitivity in staff meetings, or ask someone from a community agency that provides services to people with a specific disability such as epilepsy to come to a staff meeting so you can all learn accurate information about that condition.

❑ Invite people with various disabilities to speak informally to help employees update their knowledge and attitudes.

❑ Distribute pamphlets about rehabilitation agencies and invite speakers to describe their services, which may include job analysis, technical assistance in determining reasonable accommodations and referrals of trained workers.

The Bottom Line

The best way for employees to update their attitudes about people with disabilities is to work alongside a disabled colleague successfully. When a qualified person is hired, appropriate accommodations are made, an atmosphere of acceptance is created in the workplace and the experience increases chances for future success. The organization's attitude has a direct bearing on the success of all employees, and a willingness to give a qualified person with a disability the chance to be successful sets the tone.

Management Philosophy and Support

It is crucial for top managers to be aware of the ADA. Beyond that, they must articulate and support the organization's compliance with the law. This means everything from using appropriate and respectful language to not telling jokes about people with disabilities. It means talking about inclusion and involvement, not just compliance.

Systems need to be in place that make it easy for the rest of the organization to comply. Supervisors need to know where they can turn for assistance before interviewing an applicant with a disability. They need to know that they will be supported, philosophically as well as fiscally, when they make accommodations that may require extra time and energy. They need to be encouraged to hire nontraditional workers, including those with disabilities, and rewarded for any risk they may experience, not just successes.

SUPERVISOR: I hired a person with a disability once, but it didn't work out.

MANAGER: Have you ever hired a person without a disability who didn't work out? Let's look at how we can improve your chances of hiring people who have the skills your area needs.

Many employers consider new employment options such as telecommuting for employees without disabilities. These options may also prove beneficial for employees with disabilities.

Example: Telecommuting

Mike Allen was injured while playing basketball. The spinal cord injury resulted in quadriplegia. He had completed 14 years of education and worked as a buyer at Union Seed. As a buyer, he traveled a lot to maintain his contacts.

The first problem was making his home accessible so he could leave the medical rehabilitation center. Through a coordination of community resources, remodeling and a ramp were completed.

Efforts then turned toward his job. Union Seed was anxious to retain a good employee and assisted in modifying his work place, developing a system so Mike could work at home as well as at the company, and equipping a van. The company modified its facilities to make them accessible to Mike's wheelchair. They also installed a telephone system between the company and Mike's home, a computer system for his home, a calculator and a fax machine.

Mike now works as a broker, 40 hours per week, 60% of the time from home, as one of a growing number of telecommuters.

Training

One of the most important things an organization can do is provide two types of training on the Americans with Disabilities Act—disability awareness and sensitivity training, and ADA compliance training.

Sensitivity and Awareness

Most of us have had little or no experience in working with people with disabilities. We have, therefore, no frame of reference and little or no experience in communicating appropriately. We do not know how to offer and provide assistance graciously and tactfully. In addition, we have the pressure not to make a mistake that will get us into legal trouble. Our minds create fears that can make us say and do stupid things.

Most organizations have focused on ADA compliance training for policy makers, managers and supervisors. However, because of misunderstandings about the capabilities of people with disabilities, ADA compliance training meets only half the training need. Unless an organization provides disability awareness and sensitivity training, employees will be resistant to full implementation of the ADA.

Include trainers or present employees with disabilities in the training. Why? We are talking about new ways of communicating and interacting with people. This is not theoretical, textbook stuff. Trainees need to practice new behaviors, not just in role playing, but with real people to get over their misconceptions. Doing it in a nonthreatening setting will alleviate many fears.

If you are training supervisors or people who interview job applicants, be sure to include role play. Practice using a sign language interpreter if you foresee the possibility of hiring a person who is deaf. Once people have practiced in this situation, they are more comfortable and confident. Contact a local service center for deaf people for a list of registered interpreters.

Disability Awareness Training[2]

A basic tenet of diversity training is that people who are different from ourselves tend to evoke a stress response in us. This initial response results from a perceived threat to our status quo. Frequently, the response is based on a lack of information and/or misinformation. Such a reaction can cause well-intentioned behavior to be inappropriate, insensitive, ineffectual, counterproductive and illegal. Eradicating this prejudice, ignorance and discrimination is a crucial training issue for implementing the ADA.

We know that language influences how we think and act, including when we talk about disabilities and people with disabilities. The goal of language awareness is to use terms that are accurate, inclusive, empowering and sensitive. A key concept is to talk about *people,* not emphasizing their disabilities above their humanness. For example, use "person who is blind" rather than "the blind." Describe a group of "people with disabilities" rather than "the disabled." When in doubt, remember "people first."

Who Needs Training?

All company employees need disability awareness training. *Top management* needs it, because those who set corporate policy, culture and climate need to be aware of the capabilities of employees with disabilities as well as the legal implications of the ADA.

The human resource department needs it, because HR departments, entrusted with ensuring compliance with labor laws like the ADA, must understand the laws, communicate essential elements to the organization, ensure compliance and handle mistakes.

People involved in hiring need information about specific disabilities, appropriate (and legal) interviewing skills, types of accommodations and employment issues for people who are disabled. Most of all, they must be comfortable interacting with people who are disabled.

The HR department must ensure that all training complies with the law. For example, HR departments should provide to the training department details about the essential functions involved in the job description that a person with a disability is expected to perform.

The HR department must review the ADA regarding confidential medical information to ensure that the privacy rights of people with disabilities are honored in training sessions. Other issues the HR department may need to address include:

❑ How employees are advised of their rights under the ADA

❑ How trainers, managers and supervisors are advised of their responsibilities mandated by the ADA

❑ Resources available from outside the organization that could assist in determining and providing accommodations required by the ADA

Managers and supervisors need disability awareness training for two key issues, legal and functional. First, managers and supervisors must know the laws and regulations (like the ADA) governing the employment of people with disabilities. Managers need specific solutions to ADA requirements. Second, managers and supervisors must create a work environment that fosters employee motivation and productivity. Those who supervise, manage, promote and fire employees need to:

- ❑ Face their own fears about being disabled in the future

- ❑ Understand what it means to be disabled

- ❑ Hear success stories about employing people with disabilities

- ❑ Know the specific workplace implications of disabilities (perceived versus real limitations)

- ❑ Be knowledgeable about types of reasonable accommodations

- ❑ Be confident about communicating with people who are disabled

- ❑ Be capable of providing effective supervision, including appropriate feedback and encouragement for professional growth, when applicable

- ❑ Help nondisabled employees develop sensitivity and professional attitudes toward people who are disabled

- ❑ Assist in career planning

- ❑ Realize that behavior based on good intentions does not always produce intended results

Coworkers also need disability awareness training to understand the abilities and needs of their disabled colleagues and be taught skills for interacting and communicating appropriately with them. Coworkers need to create an environment that supports and encourages the inclusion of their colleagues with disabilities. They must become comfortable with the person, his or her disability, accommodations and abilities to contribute.

Disability awareness training can address these concerns. Such training should cover types of disabilities and their functional limitations, language about and around people with disabilities, communication skills, understanding disability culture, offering assistance, confidentiality, role playing and involving people with disabilities in the training to help employees become comfortable.

Most organizations provide training only to "keep their people out of trouble" with the ADA. While that is important, if they do not provide sensitivity training, they are doing only half the job.

Example

An assembly-line worker recovering from an injury in Calumet City, Ill., was told by his union when he asked for a specialized chair that everyone in the factory would have to get one if he did. Disability rights experts had to explain the ADA to both the union and worried managers before the worker got what he needed.[3]

Finding Awareness Training Resources

Organizations can contract with independent consultants who are themselves disabled; however, do not assume that just because a person is disabled, he or she knows how to conduct such training. As you would with any other consultant, be sure to get references.

Employees with disabilities are often willing to share their experiences to enlighten their coworkers. Employers who have had successful experiences in employing people with disabilities might answer questions about their experiences. Many organizations that represent the interests of people with disabilities will provide training at little or no cost as a public service. Videos about employees with disabilities are available. However, videos are not good substitutes for talking to people with disabilities face to face. Such conversations help employees in an organization to recognize that people with disabilities are people first.

Training in these skills will help ensure that employees are more sensitive, will accept coworkers with disabilities more readily and make all employees more productive. While training by itself cannot eliminate stereotypes, providing training on both compliance and attitudes about people with disabilities shows commitment to incorporating qualified employees with disabilities into an organization. It helps other employees look at their attitudes and accept the changes the ADA will bring.

Communicating with Employees with Disabilities

What is appropriate when talking with disabled employees? Some hints:

Focus on work-related topics and the same things that you discuss with nondisabled employees. Remember, a person is more than a disability. The disability is unimportant unless you are discussing reasonable accommodations. Remember to include employees with disabilities in an organization's social activities, since work-related discussions often occur there.

> *One man who uses a wheelchair said,*
>
> *I wish people would meet me before they meet my disability.*

Deaf Person

Communicating with an employee who is hard of hearing or deaf may be a new experience. It is OK to admit that you need to learn.

Discuss with the person how she or he prefers to communicate. Many people with diminished hearing use a combination of methods to understand spoken language, including speech-reading and interpreting body language. This may be combined with quickly jotting down key words or phrases. People cannot understand everything you say by reading your lips. Even an excellent speechreader can accurately comprehend less than half of what is said.

To let someone who is deaf or hard of hearing know that you wish to communicate, touch the person gently on the shoulder or elbow. Ask how you should do that to avoid any misperception of your intentions. The person may prefer to have you wave your hand rather than be touched. Respect the person's wishes.

Blind Person

Do not shout at a person who is blind unless you know that the person also has a hearing impairment. Speak normally. You can ask, "Do you see what I mean?" to a person who is blind, even if the person cannot see anything. Everyone uses figures of speech such as this.

Person Who Uses a Wheelchair

It is courteous to pull up a chair, sit down and face a person who uses a wheelchair when you are having more than a brief conversation. You would not want to have to look up at everyone you speak to all day. In addition, it evens the power between the two of you.

Person with Developmental Disabilities (Mental Retardation)

Do not talk "baby talk" to employees with developmental disabilities. Break down complex instructions into small tasks. Use alternative forms of job instruction such as color coding or pictures. Ask them to repeat instructions to you or demonstrate their understanding of your instructions. Other employees who are patient and interested in seeing a developmentally disabled worker succeed can assist in providing instructions and feedback.

Understanding Disability Cultures

Having a disability is more than having a physical or mental impairment that limits daily activities. In many cases, it involves a way of life and a philosophy. It may mean belonging to an organization, such as the National Federation of the Blind. It may mean separation, such as attending a church for people who are deaf or participating in Special Olympics.

These are organizations based on similarities. All of us enjoy belonging to organizations based on our interests. Some belong to a sports league, others participate in service clubs. Each of these organizations has a culture with ceremonies, traditions and customs.

Each of these groups has a culture that we may not understand if we are an "outsider." However much we try, we cannot "belong." This may be true of an employee with a disability. There are "deaf cultures," "blind cultures" and cultures of other disability groups.

When any employee has problems on the job, you try to understand the basis for those problems to help the employee solve them. You refer them to your Employee Assistance Program or a community resource agency. It is the same with an employee with a disability. You may need to refer yourself to a group that understands disability culture. There are professional associations, such as the National Association of the Deaf, which can help you understand the culture represented by an employee who is disabled.

To find organizations that can help you, first ask employees with disabilities or look in your local telephone directory. You can also contact Independent Living Centers for people with disabilities for referrals to appropriate local organizations. The *ADA Technical Assistance Manual* lists national offices of numerous organizations.

Using Appropriate Language

What is the difference between the words "handicapped" and "disabled"?

Most people in the disability communities prefer to use the word disability when discussing physical conditions. Handicap is the barrier that society puts up, either a physical barrier that prevents a person with a mobility impairment from entering a store or an attitudinal barrier that limits a person from becoming employed. For example, "The steps handicapped the young woman, who had a disability, from getting into the building." We may have lumped people with disabilities into a group ("the handicapped"). It is better to talk about an individual, rather than assigning people to a group based on a single characteristic.

Rather than referring to someone as "the blind man," you may say, "the new accountant." It is more appropriate to refer to people by their names, but if you must identify them by a disability, you may say, "the accountant who is blind."

Why is this important? We know that language influences action, and because of negative stereotypes and expectations about people with disabilities, using inappropriate language may influence inappropriate actions. For example, referring to someone as "wheelchair-bound" creates a picture in our mind of someone who never leaves the wheelchair and may not be able to move about in the workplace. It may influence our decision about whether or not to hire the person for a job that requires travel out of the office. A wheelchair is nothing more than an assistive device that allows a person to use something other than legs to move about. If we think of it as an assistive device rather than something that "binds" someone to something, we will not make assumptions about what that device permits a person to do or not do.

Incorporating People with Disabilities into Everyday Life

In 1975, Congress passed a law called The Education of All Handicapped Children's Act. It is also called Public Law 94-142, or the "Mainstreaming Law." It was reauthorized in 1991 and is now known as the Individuals with Disabilities Education Act (IDEA).

This law offers children with disabilities an education in the "least restrictive environment," rather than automatically being sent to special schools or special classrooms. The idea is that all children, both those with disabilities and those without, could benefit from learning in the same classroom. What does this have to do with the ADA?

Children who were in first grade in 1975 were born about 1970, making them 22 in 1992, the year Title I of the ADA took effect for larger companies. They may just be entering the work force. Let's look at the groups this may affect.

Young people with disabilities educated for all or part of their schooling under this law might:

❑ Be accustomed to being with nondisabled colleagues in school activities from the classroom to the choir

❑ Have had accommodations made for their disability

❏ Know more about their rights and responsibilities under laws such as the ADA

❏ Have higher expectations of themselves and their employers

Nondisabled people who had disabled classmates may have had different, and probably more positive, experiences than those of us who grew up with no disabled classmates. They might:

❏ Be more accepting, less fearful and more aware that people with disabilities can get along and be productive

❏ Know more about accommodations

Employees in your workgroup who are parents of children with disabilities born after 1970 may also be more aware and accepting. They may:

❏ Have been active in getting their schools to accommodate their disabled child

❏ Be familiar with suppliers and funding sources of reasonable accommodation

❏ Have been creating adaptations and accommodations for their children and can be valuable resources in suggesting workplace accommodations

❏ Have a vested interest in seeing the workplace become more accessible, since their children with disabilities will someday enter the workforce

Organizations would be smart to tap the experiences and wisdom of all these people in their workforce.

Conclusion

Hopefully, after reading this chapter, you have gained insight into your own attitudes about people with disabilities, as well as those of others in your organization. You should now be able to plan to train all staff about people with disabilities as well as the letter and spirit of the ADA. You should be confident that your language is sensitive and current. You are well on your way to effectively implementing the ADA!

Hiring People with Disabilities

Employers must ensure that when they interview candidates, the space is accessible and all questions are legal and appropriate

Hiring must be done fairly, ensuring only that the best person to do the essential functions of the job is hired

Employers must use creativity to get the most out of their employees, including accommodating long-time employees who become disabled while working as well as new employees who are disabled

Title I of the ADA requires that employers not discriminate against qualified people with disabilities in any aspect of employment, including candidate search, hiring and on-the-job responsibilities. To help the reader identify areas for more effective compliance, an employer self audit taken from *An Employer's Guide to the Americans with Disabilities Act*, published by Paul, Hastings, Janofsky & Walker and the Merchants and Manufacturers Association, 1991© is quoted.

To begin, organizations will want to review general policies and procedures outlined in the Self Audit.

TIPS FOR EMPLOYER SELF AUDITS

Consider the following inquiries and actions, among others, in evaluating Title I compliance.

Documented Compliance Audit

1. Conduct and document the results of an audit for compliance with the ADA.

2. Establish a schedule of actions that must be taken to achieve compliance.

3. Designate specific person(s) responsible for each action to be taken.

4. Verify that necessary steps have been taken to achieve compliance.

Discrimination Policy and Internal Complaint Procedure

1. Adopt a policy prohibiting discrimination against individuals with a disability and other protected groups and an internal complaint procedure that covers complaints of discrimination by applicants or employees with a disability. Require prompt investigation of all complaints and communication of investigation results to the complainant.

2. Post the policy and complaint procedure on employee bulletin boards.

3. Discuss the policy and complaint procedure in employee orientation, meetings and training sessions.

4. Include the policy and complaint procedure in any employee handbook of personnel policy manual.

Disability Expert

1. Designate an ADA expert (either an employee or consultant) who is well versed on: (a) the provisions of the ADA; (b) the auxiliary aids or services available to assist individuals

with a disability; (c) the special or modified equipment that allows accommodation of individuals with a disability and (d) job restructuring methods and other steps that facilitate such accommodation.

2. Establish relationships with organizations serving individuals with a disability, for recruiting, advice and other purposes and with the Job Accommodation Network for advice on reasonable accommodations.

3. Consider establishing an ADA advisory group or task force that includes representatives from the disabled community to advise the employer on workplace issues affecting that community. Such a group can provide useful suggestions, and outreach efforts of this kind doubtless would be well received publicly. However, such a group might make well-meaning but impractical suggestions, and a written record of solicitation and rejection of suggestions might be created.

Supervisor Awareness Training

1. Provide information (through training or written materials) to supervisors about the ADA. Make them sensitive to the needs of individuals with a disability and aware of the sanctions for noncompliance.

2. Advise supervisors that there is, at least theoretically, a possibility of individual liability for ADA violations.

3. Instruct supervisors to refer to the ADA expert all inquiries and potentially adverse employment decisions.

Notices and Recordkeeping

1. Post notices describing the provisions of the ADA in the employment lobby and on employee bulletin boards. Procure copies of the EEOC's 1992 poster to meet this requirement.

2. Review personnel records, maintenance policies and practices to ensure that personnel and employment records are maintained for at least one year from the date the

record is made or the personnel action is taken, whichever is later. (Retention of records for three years is preferable in case they are needed to rebut charges of age or other discrimination for which a three-year limitations period applies to willful violations.)

Facilities

1. Audit each facility to ensure it complies with the applicable Title III requirements—regardless of whether the duty to accommodate any individual arises.

Stop here and make a list of tasks you need to accomplish and who should do them. This will become part of your compliance plan.

Continue working through the self audit. Note on your compliance plan the items you need to accomplish as you proceed.

Prehire Responsibilities

Areas where you meet applicants must be accessible to people with physical disabilities, including those who use wheelchairs or have other mobility impairments. In addition, major changes are required in the way most people assess applicants.

EMPLOYER SELF AUDIT

Applications and Pre-employment Inquiries

1. Review recruiting advertisements, literature, standards and presentations for ADA compliance.

2. Review job application and other pre-employment forms. Eliminate, for example, questions relating to disability status and workers' compensation. Note the employer's EEO/nondiscrimination policy for individuals with a disability.[1]

Interview Questions

Interviewers may not ask questions about a person's perceived or actual disability. Questions may investigate only a person's ability to perform the "essential functions" of a job. This means that organizations should conduct a job analysis of each job and list the essential functions of the job before advertising any opening, as well as training all who interview about legal and useful questions.

EMPLOYER SELF AUDIT

1. Train interviewers on questions they are permitted to ask (about ability to perform job-related functions) and questions they are prohibited from asking (about the existence, nature or severity of any disability).[2]

Reasonable Accommodation

If a person indicates a need for reasonable accommodation during the application process, the company is required to provide it. A person who is deaf can request that an interpreter be hired at company expense for the interview. If hired, the company also may be responsible for providing reasonable accommodations on the job, unless doing so would present an undue hardship for the company.

Testing

If employment tests are used, they must be relevant to the essential functions of the job and must be given in alternative formats for people who cannot test in the usual fashion.

Assessing Applicants' Ability to Do the Job

The purpose of reviewing a person's application is to determine whether the person is qualified to do the job. There are many ways, in addition to the traditional interview, to get accurate information.

The ADA Says...

"Qualified" means that a person has the requisite education, training, licenses, background and experience to do the job.

This is the goal in assessing any person, disabled or not. A company tries to identify one candidate who stands out among all of them.

Effectively assessing any job applicant is both an art and a science. The organization is trying to find someone who can:

❑ Perform specific job tasks

❑ Fit into the organizational culture

❑ Get along well as a team player

❑ Be punctual and regular in attendance

❑ Be pleasant about doing what needs to be done

Depending on the job and the state of the economy, you may have more applicants than you can possibly interview, or not enough who have the skills you seek. You want to get the best person as fast as possible.

How often do you find the perfect candidate? Even after reviewing many resumes, you may not find the one person who meets all your needs. Almost all people will require some training and some period of adjustment. Coworkers may have difficulty accepting a new team member, especially one who does not fit the mold of previous team members. Do not let the presence of a disability influence your decision making or the way you evaluate an applicant with a disability.

In addition to the traditional interview, you will want to use other legal and effective methods to determine a person's appropriateness for a job. These include checking references, including school references for people with little or no work experience; internships; testing; on-the-job evaluations and job tryouts.

List three ways to assess a person's ability to do your job.

1. _____

2. _____

3. _____

Conducting Interviews

If interviewers for your organization have not attended training on interviewing practices and laws, they should. Interviewing can be a minefield of problems, not only those related to disability. The Equal Employment Opportunity Commission has prepared general guidelines of acceptable and unacceptable interview questions. The HR department should also provide guidance to all who interview.

What if two candidates are equally qualified? Must we hire the person with the disability over the other?

The answer in this case is no. The ADA is not an *affirmative action* law. It is a *nondiscrimination* law, which requires only that we not discriminate on the basis of our perceptions about a person's disability.

However, it is difficult to imagine that two human beings are exactly the same. If two people appear to have the same background, education and experience, then you would need to determine which one will "fit" the requirements of the job better. You can ask the two candidates questions that will demonstrate their differences in problem solving, communication or other job-related skills. You can ask open-ended questions such as, "I have several well-qualified candidates for this job. Please tell me what you bring to this job that would make you the person I should hire." You can also ask questions such as, "What would your past employer say if we asked what your greatest contribution to the organization was?" Be sure that your questions remain job-related and not disability-related.

Be careful in interviewing people who are new to the job market or who may not have worked since the onset of a disability. The new person may not have a significant track record to refer to, and the newly disabled person may have changed significantly since the last job.

In addition to not questioning people about their present disabilities, you cannot ask about previous workers' compensation claims, history of hospitalizations or past substance abuse. You may not ask how often a person will need to be absent for medical care. However, you can state your company's attendance policies and ask if the person can meet them.

Group Interviewing

Perhaps work teams interview candidates. In this case, they must be trained about which questions are appropriate and helpful and which are irrelevant. Moreover, one person asking one illegal question can put the company in jeopardy for a lawsuit. Team members also need to become aware of the need for increased confidentiality about candidates.

Teams can legally ask candidates about how they solve problems, how they work in a team and what their leadership experiences have been. A good question may be to ask how the candidate determines the success of a work team.

Work teams are designed to brainstorm and solve problems. If a person has lived with a disability for a long time, he or she has probably had ample experience in evaluating situations and determining appropriate ways to cope with them, a skill that the team would find valuable.

Medical Exams

During the interview, no reference can be made to a person's disability. To protect people with disabilities from discrimination, however, the ADA has specific requirements about when medical examinations may be done and the handling of the results. The ADA forbids medical examinations until after a conditional offer of employment has been made. However, an offer of employment can be made contingent upon a person passing a job-related physical exam.

EMPLOYER SELF AUDIT

Medical Examinations and Inquiries

1. State on the job application form that any job offer is contingent on successful completion of a medical examination, substance test or other screening, if required.

2. Develop structured post-offer medical questionnaires and examinations to ensure consistent treatment of persons with and without disabilities.

3. Require that, if medical examinations are used for any prospective employee in the classification, they are given to all such prospective employees.

---

4. Explain the physical and mental requirements of the employer's positions to physicians conducting medical examinations. (Physicians may find helpful written job descriptions and a videotape of job performance or observation of incumbents.)

5. Establish a medical examination report format that requires the examining physician to specify the tasks that the individual cannot perform at all, specify the tasks that the individual can perform only by posing a direct threat (i.e., a significant risk of substantial harm to self or others). Report only job-related information and transmit the report to the designated ADA expert who will make the final decision after exploring reasonable accommodations. It is desirable for the physician to specify the medical and other factual bases for his or her conclusions. Do not, however, allow the physician to make the final employment decision. That should be made only after knowledgeable persons evaluate possible accommodations.

6. Where the examining physician or ADA expert determines that an individual would pose a direct threat in performing the essential functions of a job, include in the medical report form a thorough, nonconclusory analysis of:

    a. The duration of the risk

    b. The nature and severity of the potential harm

    c. The likelihood the potential harm will occur

    d. The imminence of the potential harm, and

    e. Whether any accommodation would eliminate the risk or reduce it to an acceptable level.

7. Review medical examinations required of employees to be sure they are either voluntary or job-related and consistent with business necessity, and used to determine whether the individual can perform the essential functions of the job.

8. Review policies and practices regarding medical information to ensure it is retained on separate forms and in separate files, treated as a confidential medical record and disclosed only as permitted by the ADA and other laws.

The ADA affects the way companies give medical exams, as well as how physicians report their findings. In addition to the suggestions in the self audit, the company form may also indicate which essential functions the applicant should be able to perform without accommodation.

Direct Threat

The purpose of medical testing is to determine whether the applicant can perform the essential functions of the job without a direct threat to health or safety. If an employer uses medical examinations, the ADA requires:[4]

❏ All applicants for the same job category must undergo such an exam.

❏ The employer may not reject a job applicant for physical disabilities unless it can demonstrate that medical restrictions on *specific* activities or job-condition exposures interfere with the performance of *essential* job functions.

❏ The employer that rejects an applicant because of a disability must be prepared to demonstrate that medical restrictions on that applicant cannot be reasonably accommodated.

"These requirements mean that employers should not accept a medical report that contains the misleading phrase 'qualified with restrictions.' The employer, not the physician, must determine whether the applicant is qualified for the job by considering what is reasonable for the business to accommodate. The role of the company's medical consultant is to suggest additional training, physical conditioning, use of mechanical aids or minor alterations in the working environment that the employer might make to provide reasonable accommodation," said one doctor.[5]

To help doctors, employers should provide job descriptions that define physical requirements much more specifically than in the past. Examples would be:

> *"Must climb 20-foot wooden poles, balance on one foot for up to 60 seconds, accurately differentiate navy blue from black wiring, exert 15 pounds of grip strength and repetitively twist wrists."*[6]

Drug and Alcohol Issues

The ADA specifically mentions that drug screening is *not* considered a medical exam and *is* allowed under the ADA. However, organizations should notice how the ADA affects drug and alcohol issues. The following summarizes the key related points:[7]

1. *The ADA clearly protects recovering alcoholics and former drug addicts from discrimination.* Employers should not make any employment decision based on an employee's history of alcoholism or drug addiction. Employers also have an affirmative obligation to reasonably accommodate qualified employees or applicants who are recovering alcoholics or former drug addicts.

2. *The ADA does not protect those who illegally use drugs or alcohol.* Employers can still take action against applicants or employees who illegally use drugs. Employers may take action against applicants or employees using alcohol when the alcohol use adversely affects the employee's ability to perform the essential functions of the job or the individual does not otherwise have a disability.

3. *The ADA greatly limits employer inquiries into prescription medications.* Under the ADA, employers may not inquire into an employee's physical or mental condition or disability, except in limited circumstances, including questions about prescription medications. Consequently, employers may not require employees to alert their supervisors to their prescription use, as is common in many substance abuse policies. Furthermore, employers should no longer ask employees to identify prescription or over-the-counter drug

use on drug testing consent forms. Rather, for employees, those inquiries should be made only by a medical review officer for confirmation of a positive test result.

4. *Drug testing should follow a conditional job offer.* These limitations on inquiries into prescription drug use also apply to applicants before a conditional job offer is extended. Consequently, employers should conduct any drug testing after the conditional job offer so that the employer (or medical review officer) can inquire into prescription medications to verify a positive test result.

5. *The ADA severely limits alcohol testing.* Alcohol testing is considered a "medical examination" under the ADA. An employer can require medical examinations for applicants, but only after extending a conditional job offer, and for employees, but only when the employee has difficulty performing the job effectively, has provided notice of a disability or has requested a disability accommodation. Consequently, employers should screen for alcohol use only upon reasonable suspicion, after accidents and conditional job offers. Random alcohol testing violates the ADA.

6. *The ADA can limit an employer's actions after a positive alcohol screen.* Because alcohol is a legal drug, employers should not take action automatically against applicants or employees who test positive for the presence of alcohol. Action should be taken only when the use of alcohol adversely affects the employee's performance of the job or where there is no indication that the employee has a disability such as alcoholism or drug addiction. Generally, when the alcohol screen is used in cases of reasonable suspicion or postaccident situations, alcohol use has already affected job performance. Consequently, this limitation will be most significant for positive pre-employment alcohol screens.

No doubt, many employers will be surprised by this list of ways their substance abuse policy may be affected by the ADA. Congress may be surprised as well, as some of the effects may be unintended consequences of the law. Nevertheless, each employer should review its substance abuse policy to ensure compliance with the ADA. To be safe, you may want to review it with your attorney.

Confidentiality

The ADA requires a higher degree of confidentiality than in the past. Any results of medical tests and any information about a person's disability must be kept in a separate locked location with limited access.

Hiring Qualified People With Disabilities

When you have job openings in your organization, how are they filled? Does Human Resources have a current, accurate, written job description that defines the essential functions of the job? Good!

Do you have an idea of the "type" of person you hire? Does that preconception rule out people who are in any way different from those who are in your work group? The ADA does not require that you give preference to or hire a person with a disability; however, you can expand your horizons, keeping an open mind about people you hire.

Concentrate on what needs to be accomplished and the skills someone needs, not personality or physical characteristics. For example, if you have an opening for a front-desk receptionist, rather than asking for a "young, pleasant-appearing person," you can say: "need front-office receptionist who makes our customers and clients feel welcome." That specifies the results you want (customers feeling welcome) rather than the type of person you think can do that.

TIPS FOR SELF AUDIT

Job Requirements and Descriptions

1. Review job requirements, particularly physical requirements such as sitting, standing or the successful completion of certain tests, to ensure they are job related for the position and are consistent with business necessity.

2. Before advertising or recruiting for a position, develop a comprehensive written job description that describes all

---

duties the employer believes are "essential functions" of the job. When in doubt, err on the side of inclusion.

    a. Include attendance as well as qualitative and quantitative performance standards.

    b. Include sensory and physical requirements in describing essential functions. For example: "Use full range of peripheral vision to operate fork lift," "Read government procurement contracts," "Lift 50-pound bags to shoulder level repetitively throughout the work shift," and "Answer office telephones and communicate information to callers."

    c. State that "the essential functions of the position include, but are not limited to. . . ."

    d. As the final job duty, list: "other functions that may be assigned."

    e. Indicate that "management retains the discretion to add to or change the duties of the position at any time."

3. Have incumbents and supervisors verify the accuracy of each job description. Include on each description a statement that the incumbent and supervisor have carefully reviewed the content and believe it to be accurate, followed by lines for their signatures and the date.

4. Have the ADA expert approve each job description.

5. Explicitly rescind all existing job descriptions that are not current and do not meet the desired level of specificity.

6. Establish a system to revise job descriptions as jobs change.

7. If it is not possible to ensure job descriptions are thorough, do not create or maintain any job descriptions.[8]

Job Analysis and Job Descriptions

The key to success with the ADA is understanding the concept of essential functions. The easiest way is to look at your own job. Imagine that you have been selected for a promotion and you are preparing to hire your successor.

■ ■

Exercise

Answer the following.

1. My job exists to accomplish the following tasks: _____

   _____

   _____

2. I was hired for my expertise in _____

   _____

   _____

3. The tasks I spend most of my time doing are _____

   _____

   _____

4. My most important duties are _____

   _____

   _____

5. If I did not do the tasks listed above, this is what would happen: _____

   _____

   _____

6. Other duties I perform but which someone else could do are _____

_____

_____

The tasks you list under items 1–5 above would be considered "essential functions" under the ADA, while those in item 6 would be "marginal." The ADA requires that an applicant be able to perform the essential functions of a job, with or without reasonable accommodation.

■ ■

Job Analysis

What you have just done is complete the first part of a "job analysis." You will need to analyze all jobs and incorporate your analysis in the job descriptions. In addition to identifying essential and marginal functions, complete the following for your own job.

Physical requirements _____

_____

_____

Mental requirements _____

_____

_____

Working conditions _____

_____

_____

Level of responsibility _____

_____

_____

Layout of work station and building _____

_____

_____

Equipment used to do the job; i.e., milling machine, carpenter's tools, computer, laboratory equipment _____

_____

_____

This exercise gets you started thinking about jobs so you can logically review them to determine their components. Then you can hire someone who will be successful.

More complete methods of conducting job analysis include using checklists or computer programs. Now, using the essential functions you wrote, develop a job announcement for your job.

■■

Job Announcement Exercise

Job title: _____

What results do you expect? _____

What are the essential functions of the job? _____

_____

_____

_____

What education, certification or licenses are required? _____

_____

_____

What must the person do to apply? _____

_____

_____

■ ■

Posting Job Announcements

The ADA requires that announcements be available and accessible to all applicants. Check to ensure that yours are at a height where anyone can access them, that they are in a language that all employees can understand and that they are available to people who do not read well. If job announcements are available only in written format and the job does not require reading, you may be discriminating unwittingly against someone who doesn't read. You may put them on tape or in a voice mail box or have someone available to read them aloud. Make sure, also, that you have posted the appropriate ADA notices, either in your employment office or department, as required by the ADA.

There is more to recruiting potential employees, but we will assume that your human resources department uses community organizations and schools to identify qualified candidates with disabilities.

Accommodating the Employee with a Disability

Enhancing employee productivity through accommodation

Financing reasonable accommodations for employees with disabilities

Determining what is a reasonable accommodation

Once a qualified person with a disability is hired, the employer needs to consider another key to successful ADA implementation, the issue of reasonable accommodation.

You are only required to accommodate a known disability, and only if the qualified person with a disability requests accommodation. You are not expected to diagnose a disability.

Enhancing Employee Productivity through Accommodation

How do we enhance our employees' ability to do their job?

❑ We purchase equipment that increases productivity, such as word processors instead of typewriters

❑ We offer chairs with back supports to workers who must sit all day

❑ We may provide flextime to accommodate the needs of working parents

❑ We offer Employee Assistance Programs to help workers handle personal problems

Some workplace modifications cost almost nothing, while others are expensive. However, we consider the employees' health and welfare to be crucial in their ability to meet our needs as employers. We absorb the cost as a cost of doing business.

What do you presently do to enhance worker productivity in your organization? _____

_____

_____

The same philosophy applies to providing reasonable accommodations for workers with disabilities. The purpose of accommodating qualified people with disabilities is to enhance their abilities so that, despite the disability, they are productive. We need only to accommodate limitations in their ability to perform the essential functions of the job.

It is important to remember that many employees with disabilities require no accommodations other than attitudinal adjustments on the part of employers and coworkers.

For those who require more extensive accommodation, here is a process.

EMPLOYER SELF AUDIT

Reasonable Accommodation Procedures and Documentation of Adverse Decisions

1. Establish and implement a procedure to comply with the ADA's reasonable accommodation requirement, in which an individual with a disability cannot perform job functions safely or at all without accommodation.

    a. Require that the ADA expert explore with the individual the job tasks or work environment that limit the individual's ability to perform.

    b. Explore with the candidate whether any reasonable accommodation would allow the individual to perform the essential functions safely.

    c. Identify potential accommodations in consultation with the individual and outside experts.

    d. Assess the reliability and effectiveness of each potential accommodation in facilitating safe and successful job performance in a timely manner.

    e. Consider the individual's preference before selecting and implementing the chosen accommodation.

    f. Explore resources of funding for potential accommodation, if required.

g. Determine whether any or all of the potential accommodations would constitute an undue hardship (i.e., significant difficulty or expense).

h. Offer the accommodation the individual prefers, if reasonable. If not, offer an alternate, reasonable accommodation.

i. Document the accommodation offered and the individual's response to it/them.

j. Note the projected or actual costs of accommodation offered to, but rejected by, the individual, and what portion of the costs the employer offered to pay.

k. If no accommodation is offered that the individual finds acceptable, document in nonconclusory terms, with specifics, the reasons that any accommodation declined by the employer either would not have allowed the individual to perform essential functions or would have imposed an undue hardship on the operation of the employer's business (i.e., significant difficulty or expense). Document such items as the problems that will be caused by the accommodation, the effect on other employees or the public, the consequences or efficiency loss the accommodation would cause and the cost of this and other accommodations made during the year in relation to the facility's overall budget.

2. Keep records of all accommodations made to establish the reasonableness of the employer's actions, support claims of undue hardship based on cumulative expense and foster consistency. (Past actions may establish a standard for future cases.)

3. Document the legitimate, nondiscriminatory bases for adverse decisions affecting an individual with a disability and applicable defenses. Retain documents that prove the facts on which the determination is based.

4. Tell the candidate exactly why a job offer was withdrawn or other adverse decision was made, to prevent misunderstanding and facilitate reconsideration if the employer's understanding of the facts was erroneous.

Financing Accommodations

It is the employer's responsibility to provide reasonable accommodation for employees with disabilities. Before considering accommodations to be an "undue hardship," learn about several options to assist in paying for them.

Disabled Access Credit (Section 44 of the Internal Revenue Code)

If you are a small business, defined as "any person whose gross receipts did not exceed $1 million for the preceding taxable year, or who employed not more than 30 fulltime employees during the preceding year," you may be eligible for the Disabled Access Credit (DAC) found in Section 11611 of OBRA 1990, which established Section 44 of the IRS Code of 1986.

DAC equals 50% of the "eligible access expenditures" that exceed $250 but do not exceed $10,250, for a maximum credit of $5,000 a year. Eligible access expenditures are "amounts paid or incurred by an eligible small business for the purpose of enabling small businesses to comply with applicable requirements" of the ADA. An eligible small business may deduct the difference between the DAC claimed and the disabled access expenditures incurred, up to $15,000, under Section 190, provided such expenditures are eligible for the Section 190 deduction.

Expenditures may include:

❏ Removing architectural, communication, physical or transportation barriers

❏ Providing qualified interpreters or other methods of making aurally delivered materials available to individuals with hearing impairments

❏ Providing qualified readers, taped texts and other methods of making visually delivered materials available to individuals with visual impairments

❑ Acquiring or modifying equipment or devices

❑ Providing other similar services, modifications, materials or equipment

All expenditures must be "reasonable" and meet the standards of the IRS with the concurrence of the Architectural and Transportation Barriers Compliance Board. Expenses incurred for new construction are not eligible.

For more information, contact a local IRS office or:

> Mark Pitzer, Attorney
> Office of Chief Counsel
> Internal Revenue Service
> 1111 Constitution Ave. NW
> Washington, DC 20224
> (202) 566-3292

Agency Assistance

Some qualified people with disabilities will look for a job while in active client status with the state Division of Vocational Rehabilitation or Commission for the Blind. Sometimes the plan to help the person become employed will include funds for providing job-related equipment or other services to the employer.

Vendor Discounting

Occasionally vendors will offer discounts on equipment to qualified individuals with disabilities. The employee may know about this, but it wouldn't hurt for you to ask your vendors.

Health Insurance Benefits

Some health insurance companies will cover the cost of assistive devices.

Example: Injured Employee Returns to Work

An insurance company asked JAN (the Job Accommodation Network) for information to help a furniture refinisher get back to work after a leg injury. The worker had been receiving physical therapy for three months, but the injury left him unable to bend and kneel frequently while working on furniture of different shapes and weights. JAN suggested a flat lift table known as a "liftmat." This piece of equipment could elevate the furniture to a height that enabled the worker to sit or stand while working. The insurance company was pleased to pay for the equipment that not only helped the employee return to work but also eliminated its disability payments.[1]

The Person with the Disability

You are not allowed to ask the employee to pay for needed accommodations. However, a person may have equipment that was used in a previous job, or may even offer to pay for part of the costs. If the person offers, you may accept.

Accommodation is a collaborative process between the employee and the supervisor. Do not automatically assume that an employee with a disability needs accommodation or that accommodations must be fancy or expensive. In each case, consider job duties, work environment, limitations imposed by the disability, other employees doing the same job, safety issues and financial implications.

Type of Accommodation

The first step is to insure that an employee with a mobility impairment can get into the building and access the work area. Beyond that, the ADA specifies several of types of accommodation:

Job restructuring. Pat, a file clerk who is deaf, cannot answer the telephone; therefore she takes on additional duties, such as ordering office supplies, while another clerk answers the phone.

Example: Accommodation

A 56-year-old production bottling line employee suffered a disabling back injury while working as a canister washer, resulting in limited pushing and pulling capacity. As a canister washer, he needed to constantly bend and twist and lift canisters into the wash as well as remove clean canisters and place them on a pallet.

The conveyor system leading up to the washer was powered and raised 27 inches. The power eliminated the necessity for the worker to push or pull pallets to the washer. Raising the system placed the pallet in a waist-high position so the worker did not have to bend to retrieve the canisters.

Part-time or modified work schedule. Diego, a wheelchair user, comes to work one-half hour earlier (or later) than other employees to take advantage of accessible public transportation.

Reassignment to a vacant position. Dale, an employee injured on the job, returns to the same company, but in a different job.

Acquisition or modification of equipment or devices. Kieko, a drafter who uses a wheelchair, needs her desk raised so her wheelchair will fit under it. A 2 × 4 is placed under each leg of her desk. This may make the desk surface too high, so additional adjustments are made to keep the workstation ergonomically correct.

Example: Accommodation

Accommodating a hearing impaired person can be as simple as making environmental modifications—for example, a company could improve acoustics and lighting to avoid interference with hearing aids and to make lip-reading easier. Other devices, such as visual and tactile signaling devices, vibrotactile beeping pagers, fire alarm and smoke detector signalers and doorbell and telephone alerting devices, might be needed.

Sign language interpreters, who charge between $25–$60 per hour, may be necessary for pre-employment interviews, staff meetings and training seminars. The most common "extra" is a TDD (telecommunication device for the deaf), which costs about $200.

Example: Sample Accommodations and Costs

❏ Providing a drafting table, page turner and pressure-sensitive tape recorder for a sales agent paralyzed from a broken neck ($950).

❏ Changing a desk layout from the right to the left side for a data entry operator who had a shoulder injury ($0).

❏ Supplying a telephone amplifier for a computer programmer who was hard of hearing ($56).

❏ Providing a special chair for a district sales agent to alleviate pain caused by a back injury ($400).

❏ Providing padded wrist rests under a computer keyboard to alleviate strain of repetitive motion and carpal tunnel syndrome ($35).[2]

Example: Accommodation

A 32-year-old truck driver was involved in an auto accident resulting in a disabling back injury. As a result, he could sit for only 30 minutes at a time, while the job required sitting for up to two hours while driving over rough terrain with continuous bouncing and jarring.

The company purchased an Air Ride seat, which minimized the jarring through special construction, including an adjustable lumbar support, air shock and scissors suspension. As a result, 75% of the bouncing was absorbed and he was able to maintain his job.

Example: Accommodation

A 44-year-old warehouse worker sustained an industrial injury to his back, resulting in reduced walking and bending ability. The job required the worker to sort damaged and returned goods from a pallet at floor level and then place them in 48-inch-high cardboard bins. Once the bins were filled, the worker used a manual pallet jack to remove bins to the appropriate work area.

A lift truck was purchased so that the worker would not be required to bend down to sort damaged goods. It allowed the worker to work at a comfortable height. The lift truck also allows the worker to move the bins while sitting, rather than walking when operating the manual pallet jacks.

Example: Accommodation

A 32-year-old truck driver/plant mechanic sustained a back injury in an on-the-job auto accident, resulting in a limitation to lifting and carrying no more than 100 pounds. His job required driving tank trucks to a distribution center and off-loading 55-gallon drums of petroleum products, stacked two high, weighing more than 500 pounds.

The company purchased a ROL lift and barrel-lift attachment to allow the worker to off-load 55-gallon drums without manually lifting.

Example: Accommodation

A logger sustained an injury to his hip resulting in a sitting limitation of 1-1/2 hours at a time. He could not return to his job as a logger, so became an insurance adjuster.

He used a versatility table, which allowed him to adjust the table height so he could either sit or stand to do his job.

Example: Accommodation

A 37-year-old bagger operator with a fruit and nut company injured her right wrist, then underwent surgery for carpal tunnel, resulting in limited use of the right hand for grasping, squeezing, pushing, pulling and fine finger manipulation.

She was unable to return to her old job, but became a receptionist/lab assistant, where she was required to fill test tube vials with a solution by means of a manual spring-loaded syringe. This required squeezing. The company purchased a pipetting machine that automatically pumps the solution into vials, eliminating the use of the spring-loaded syringe.

Adjustment or modification of examinations, training materials or policies. Olaf, a management trainee who has diabetes, attends a week-long training program. He must eat small snacks and administer his insulin on a regular basis, so he is provided a small ice chest and regularly scheduled breaks.

Provision of qualified readers or interpreters. A secretary reads daily mail to Tan, a blind computer programmer. An interpreter serves so a deaf employee can participate fully in staff meetings.

Other, similar accommodations for individuals with disabilities. Susan, who is undergoing treatment for breast cancer, leaves early one day a week for chemotherapy treatments.

If you have quality improvement teams and if the employee with a disability is willing, team members may brainstorm ways to accommodate the disability. This is just a different use of problem solving and managing for quality.

You might find that an accommodation for one person's disability helps other employees improve productivity. It may also help customers and others who do business with you. For example, installing a ramp for a wheelchair user makes it easier for delivery people and parents with baby strollers. Ramps are also easier to shovel after a snowstorm than steps.

Procedure for Determining Reasonable Accommodations[3]

Once an employee and employer have decided that a reasonable accommodation will permit the employee to perform the essential functions of a job, what steps should be taken to determine the appropriate accommodation?

In addition to the procedures outlined in the Employer Self Audit, try this four-step plan.

1. Ask the employee. As the person most familiar with the disability's ramifications, the employee may be in the best position to offer suggestions. In addition, the ADA encourages people with disabilities to be major decision makers.

2. Ask the supervisor, the person whose responsibility it is to help all employees be most productive.

3. Evaluate the work site. It may be useful to hire an expert who could address these factors.

   a. Analysis of job tasks

      Identify specific tasks necessary to complete the job, step by step.

Analyze tools and equipment. Look at necessary physical demands.

Watch someone else. The person who is most productive has developed effective work methods and may inspire ideas to help the person with the disability.

Try it yourself with the limitation experienced by the employee with the disability.

Determine the crucial task: which component of the job causes difficulty?

b. Functional assessment. Identify the employee's abilities, including motor skills, cognitive abilities, learning style and motivation. This may lead to ways to accommodate on that particular job, or may indicate skills that can be used in a different job.

c. Assess the work environment.

Proper positioning: seating, tool location, desks, lights, etc.

External stimulus: noise, lighting, fumes, etc.

Architectural barriers: immediate work area, cafeteria, parking, etc.

d. Barrier identification

Identify problems and task-related behaviors such as specifications for speed, efficiency and accuracy.

e. Understand employer concerns such as perceptions of others (don't discriminate based on this, but defuse it); protection from liability (document the process used to determine reasonable accommodation).

f. Scope of accommodations

Accommodations must be necessary and appropriate, but do not have to be the most expensive or extensive available. If there is a dispute over accommodation, bring in an outside expert. Document both successful and unsuccessful accommodations.

4. Problem resolution strategies

Try alternative methods. Changing the way a task is done is usually the easiest and cheapest way to accommodate. As long as the task is completed with required accuracy, it may not matter how it is accomplished.

Job restructuring: Share duties with another employee.

Modify the environment: Identify existing technology, modify existing technology or create new technology (only as a last resort).

Use this strategy to work through the accommodation process. You will find that it brings out the best in people.

Commonly Asked Questions About Reasonable Accommodation

Is Permitting Excessive Absences a Form of Accommodation?

In a recent ruling (U.S. District Court for the District of Columbia case: Carr v. Barr, 59, Empl. Prac. Dec. (CCH) Para. 41, 651; June 23, 1992), the U.S. District Court for the District of Columbia found that regular attendance is an essential function of the job and an employee is not otherwise qualified to perform the job when that essential function cannot be met. This case is significant, because, although it was based on the Rehabilitation Act of 1973, it may be a forerunner of decisions concerning reasonable accommodation under the ADA.

The process of determining accommodations underscores the importance of having a good job description and outlining attendance responsibilities as an essential function.

When Does Accommodation Become "Unreasonable" Rather than "Reasonable"?

The ADA does not identify a dollar amount to spend on accommodations, nor does it define specifically what is "reasonable."

As with all other aspects of the ADA, it depends on individual circumstances. Some "reasonable" accommodations may involve the purchase of equipment or modification of a workstation. More difficulty arises when an employee with a progressive medical condition, such as severe arthritis or AIDS, needs more and more assistance or longer periods of time off for medical treatment.

Some ideas:

❏ Make sure that the employee understands the requirement to perform the essential functions of the job, including attendance requirements.

❏ Document discussions you and the employee have had about accommodations.

❏ If absences become burdensome, look at the possibility of switching to parttime work. Also consider allowing the employee to work at home or telecommute, with occasional time in the office. With modems and fax machines becoming more common, this may be reasonable.

❏ Involve the employee in decision making at every step in the process, including when "reasonable" becomes "unreasonable."

Applying Creativity and Adaptability

A key criteria for success in hiring and enhanced employee productivity is creativity. Unknown situations, whether they are new equipment purchase policies or human resource initiatives, require the ability to look at opportunities from a new perspective. Let's consider a fun yet practical application of the principles of reasonable accommodation.

Case Study #1

You have been invited to the home of a new business colleague who has recently arrived from Japan. A delicious meal is set in front of you by your Japanese hostess, and your only implement is a pair of chopsticks. You have never before eaten with chopsticks. You do not want to embarrass yourself or your hostess. You pick up your chopsticks and casually try to grasp the bite-sized pieces of food. You cannot make the chopsticks work effectively.

Case Study Review

How might you feel in a situation like this when you are hungry, helpless and you do not want to embarrass yourself? What do you do? First, think about your options. List three here.

1.

2.

3.

Then ask yourself, "What are the pros and cons of each alternative?"

Option 1. *Pros* _____

_____

Cons _____

_____

Option 2. *Pros* _____

_____

Cons _____

_____

Option 3. *Pros* _____

_____

Cons _____

_____

Let's review some options.

❑ Ask your hostess or host for assistance. Your hostess demonstrates, first showing you how to place the bottom chopstick in your hand and then the second chopstick above it. Then she shows you how to wiggle the top chopstick and pick up your food. You try it and find that you are very awkward.

❑ You consider using your fingers but realize that is unacceptable.

❑ You ask for a fork, but your hostess has just moved from Japan and has no Western-style eating instruments in the house.

❑ Your hostess has foreseen the potential problem and brings out a rubber band and a folded piece of paper. She places the piece of paper between the chopsticks at the top end and wraps the rubber band around the chopsticks, effectively holding them together. She then shows you how to manipulate the top chopstick to grasp the food. You eat the delicious meal, although you still feel somewhat uncoordinated. You let your embarrassment pass and enjoy the experience.

Consider your feelings about yourself and your hostess in this last option. Although you may feel somewhat embarrassed, you are grateful for your hostess's foresight in accommodating your needs.

Let's assume that the rubber band does not make it easier for you. You and your hostess can brainstorm together on how to solve this problem.

The desired outcome is to use two pieces of wood to pick up food. What other ways might you do it?

❏ Use one chopstick in each hand

❏ Use one of the chopsticks to pierce each bite-sized piece of food

❏ Put some sticky substance on the end that will hold the food

You might try this exercise with your staff. Get some inexpensive wooden chopsticks, pass them out at a staff meeting and ask people to modify those chopsticks so they are easier to use. Provide simple items such as paper clips, rubber bands or tape for their use. As a final exam for yourself and your staff, get some jelly beans and practice transferring them from one plate or napkin to another. When you can do this easily, you will know that you can eat anything with chopsticks.

What Does This Exercise Teach Us?

During the exercise, you were "chopstick impaired." You were unable to use the traditional tools of the job in the traditional way to accomplish the desired outcome. At first, you were clumsy and perhaps your production rate was not fast. With practice, you probably improved.

Suppose you lack coordination, have missing fingers or struggle with carpal tunnel syndrome, which would prevent you from ever using chopsticks competently in the traditional fashion. You may need to identify a modification. Perhaps the rubber band was sufficient. If not, you may need to redesign the chopsticks. You may need to use a different instrument such as a fork. You may also redesign the inspection job so that the jelly beans do not need to be picked up and transferred at all.

Similar exercises for another staff meeting:

- ❏ How many uses can you come up with for a paperclip?

- ❏ You are on your way to an important meeting and the heel on your shoe comes off; how would you fix it when you don't have time to stop at a shoe repair store?

The process of determining how to accomplish these everyday tasks is the same process you use to identify potential accommodations!

Documenting Accommodation Efforts

While not specifically required by the ADA, documenting the accommodation process and the accommodations that you provide is important because additional workers may need similar accommodations in the future, and an employee may challenge decisions not to provide additional accommodations.

Include in your documentation:

- ❏ The discussions that you have with the employee.

- ❏ The cost of various accommodations you discuss. Document why you chose the accommodation you did.

- ❏ Alternative funding sources you identify (vocational rehabilitation agencies, accommodations the employee already owns, etc.).

- ❏ Time lines on accommodations that require time away from the job.

Don't mislead the employee about making an accommodation if you are not sure it is feasible. Put your decisions in memo form to the employee so there are no misunderstandings.

Accommodating Employees Who Become Disabled

Anyone can become disabled at any time, either on or off the job. Auto accidents, sports-related injuries or just growing older provide opportunities for people to become disabled during their working years. As people work longer, more will become disabled and qualify for protection under the ADA. Most people who will be protected under the ADA are not new, but present employees. Why should you accommodate these workers?

❑ Your organization has spent time, energy and money to develop employees into productive workers.

❑ Recruiting, hiring and training new people is expensive.

❑ Accommodating employees who become disabled is time- and cost-effective.

What can you do when an employee becomes disabled? Here are some steps to take to increase the chances that an employee will return to productivity quickly.

1. Develop your organization's return-to-work policy and train all managers and supervisors about it.

2. Let the newly disabled employee know of your support.

❑ If appropriate, send flowers.

❑ It is always encouraging to say, "We miss you. What can we do to help you?"

❑ Keep in touch to enhance the person's interest in the job and coworkers.

3. Even if the person is not totally able to return to work, consider telecommuting if the job can be adapted to it. Provide equipment such as a computer, modem or fax so the person can be productive according to physical stamina.

4. Consider having the person return parttime.

Your chances for successful return are greatly increased if your organization has an early return-to-work policy and program, which encourage and enable injured or disabled employees to return to work under medical supervision before they are fully recuperated. Organizations often identify light duty positions or provide for parttime work progressing toward fulltime, which capitalizes on a person's skills without demanding full physical functioning. These organizations value retaining and retraining present employees rather than replacing them.

The ADA does not mandate an early return-to-work policy. However, depending on your ADA philosophy, you can help a valued employee get back on the job as soon as medically feasible.

When a person is able to return, either full- or parttime, review the job description to determine the essential functions and talk with the employee about which of those functions can be done without accommodation. Identify duties that will require accommodation, and ask the employee if he or she knows which accommodations are needed. If not, ask if the person is working with an occupational therapist or a vocational rehabilitation specialist. If so, with the employee's permission, involve the rehabilitation professional in performing a job analysis to determine appropriate accommodations. Then make accommodations, either by restructuring the job in-house or providing accommodations from outside vendors or resources. Do not forget to let your accounting department know about tax credits.

Additional Posthire Responsibilities

The employer has other responsibilities after hiring a person with a disability. They may not be as obvious, but they deserve attention.

Promotion

Underemployment of people with disabilities is almost as great a problem as unemployment. Supervisors may mistakenly assume that a person with a disability is happy with an entry-level job and has no aspirations beyond that. The ADA asks you to recognize a person's ambitions and offer the same opportunities for career planning and advancement as you would any employee.

If a promotion requires new forms of accommodation to allow the person with disabilities to be fully productive, you and the disabled employee will work together to determine which accommodation will meet the needs. This will give you both a chance to identify work-related issues before they become problems.

Benefits

The ADA specifically prohibits employers from discriminating against employees with disabilities in any form of compensation, benefit or condition of employment. The HR offices should maintain information about how the ADA affects compensation and benefit plans.

Organizations must offer the same benefits to all employees. Do not assume that a person with a disability would not, for example, want a health club membership just because the person uses a wheelchair. Company-run health clubs must be accessible to and useable by people with disabilities, and many people with disabilities use them for swimming, weight lifting and other activities that nondisabled people enjoy.

Insurance

Employer-paid health insurance is one of the biggest gray areas to come out of the initial ADA regulations. The EEOC, on June 8, 1993, issued *Interim Enforcement Guidance on the Application of the ADA to Disability-Based Provisions of Employer-Provided Health Insurance.* This document is available from the EEOC by calling (202) 663-4900.

There are four basic requirements.

1. Disability-based insurance distinctions are permitted only if the employer-provided health insurance plan is bona fide and if the distinctions are not being used as a subterfuge for purposes of evading the ADA.

2. Decisions about the employment of an individual with a disability cannot be motivated by concerns about the effect of the individual's disability on the employer's health plan

3. Employees with disabilities must be accorded equal access to whatever health insurance the employer provides to employees without disabilities

4. An employer cannot make an employment decision about any person, whether or not that person has a disability, because of concerns about the effect on the health plan of the disability of someone with whom that person has a relationship.

Leaves of Absence, Sick Leave and the Family and Medical Leave Act of 1993

EMPLOYER SELF AUDIT

Policies and Practices

1. Review medical leave policies to ensure that they:

    a. Permit reasonable accommodation of individuals with a disability.

    b. Require employees to submit medical documentation to support a leave request.

    c. Require employees to submit medical documentation from the treating physician authorizing release to return to work and indicating whether any restrictions apply.

    d. Reserve the right to require examination by an employer-designated physician.

    e. Enforce uniformly, for employees with and without disabilities, rules pertaining to authorizations to return to work.[5]

The Family and Medical Leave Act of 1993 (FMLA) requires employers with 50 or more employees to provide up to 12 weeks of unpaid, job-protected leave to take care of a newborn or newly adopted child, to care for a sick parent, spouse or child or because of an employee's own serious health condition. There have been some concerns about the relationship between the ADA and the FMLA.

The Department of Labor issued interim rules on June 3, 1993, to implement the FMLA. Section 825.702 states that nothing in the FMLA modifies or affects any federal or state law prohibiting discrimination. This means that if an employee is a qualified individual with a disability under the ADA, the employer must make reasonable accommodations as required under that law, but at the same time the employee must be afforded FMLA rights.

The rules provide three examples of compliance under both laws. They are quoted here from the *BNA's Americans with Disabilities Act Manual:*[6]

❏ If an employee becomes disabled, an employer might make a reasonable accommodation under the ADA by providing the employee with a parttime job with no health benefits. However, FMLA would permit an employee to work a reduced leave schedule until 12 weeks of leave is used up, with health benefits maintained during this period. At the end of the FMLA leave entitlement, the employee must be reinstated to the same or equivalent position. If the employee were unable to perform the equivalent position because of a disability, the ADA may permit or require the employer to make a reasonable accommodation by placing the employee in a parttime job, receiving only those benefits that other parttime employees receive.

❏ If an employee is entitled to leave under the FMLA, an employer may not, in lieu of leave entitlement, require an employee to take a job with a reasonable accommodation. However, under the ADA, the employer may be required to offer the employee the opportunity to take such a position.

❏ If an employer requires certification of any employee's fitness for duty to return to work as permitted by the FMLA, the employer must comply with the ADA's requirement that a fitness-for-duty physical examination be job related.

Selection and Financial Support for Training

Any training you provide to your employees must be available to people with disabilities. The training location must be accessible, and training materials may need to be adapted to a format that provides the best opportunity for learning despite a person's disability.

It is important that people with disabilities have the opportunity to attend training away from the office. If a training session is out of town or at a site away from the accessible worksite, you must ensure that it is accessible to all participants. Training-related events such as meals, to which all trainees must go, shall be accessible so that a person with a disability can be included. We all know that a lot of learning takes place over dinner and at the social events people attend together. The disabled person has a right to attend all events related to the training.

EMPLOYER SELF AUDIT

Audit training programs to ensure that the facilities at which they are offered are accessible, the materials are usable and the methods of instruction permit effective communication with individuals with a disability.[7]

Sponsored Activities such as Social and Recreational Programs

EMPLOYER SELF AUDIT

Examine company-sponsored social and recreational programs to ensure that they are accessible and nondiscriminatory to individuals with a disability.[8]

Any Other Term, Condition or Privilege of Employment

EMPLOYER SELF AUDIT

Contractual Relationships

1. Require all entities contracting with the employer to certify compliance with the ADA on all contracts with which the employer must comply.

2. Include in all contracts a clause that gives the employer a right to indemnification and damages if the contractor breaches any ADA obligation involving the employer.[9]

five

Supervising the Employee with a Disability

Enhance the performance of employees with disabilities by ensuring they have equal access to on-the-job training, informal groups, adequate feedback, and that coworkers have been sensitized to ADA issues

Companies that have successfully used the ADA to bolster their workforce have used progressive hiring and retraining practices, recognition ceremonies, videos and other techniques

Support services for employers include federal, state and local agencies as well as private, community, and individual sources

Supervising a person with a disability should not be difficult. People with disabilities come in all shapes, sizes, colors, communication styles and personalities, just like employees without disabilities. If you are faced with a supervisory situation in which you are uncertain about how to act or what to do, the rule of thumb is, use courtesy, communication and common sense.

To hire and retain disabled employees, an organization must have a culture that accepts, involves and respects all employees. Think about the tone of your organization. Circle the word in each pair that most closely describes it.

❑ Calm or hurried

❑ Creative or rule-bound

❑ Casual or formal

❑ Traditional or progressive

❑ Playful or serious

How does the organizational tone affect relationships and productivity? Do people get along well, or is there dissention? Is productivity as high as it should be?

How are people who are "different" treated? Are people accepted only for what they can do for the bottom line? Is everyone included in social events? Do people interact with everyone in the group, or only with those of the same gender, race or cultural background?

These are important considerations as the workplace becomes more diverse. To be effective, an organization and the units within it must accept and include all who contribute to the bottom line. This extends to those with physical or mental differences as well as gender or ethnic differences.

Enhancing the Performance of Employees with Disabilities

Organizations today have many tools and opportunities to support and promote top-notch performance from all employees. Let's review ways your organization can meets its goals by capitalizing on each employee's strengths and minimizing limitations.

Training

Provide adequate on-the-job training for all employees, ensuring that training materials are in accessible formats and that appropriate time is given for people to learn the job if they have a disability that makes it hard to learn from traditional materials or methods.

Providing Feedback

The ADA does not require that you lower quality or quantity standards for any employee. It is crucial to communicate your performance expectations with all employees. Workers with disabilities need feedback on their performance just like other employees, praise when appropriate and corrective counseling or coaching when needed. Do not wait until there is a serious problem. Involve the employee in problem-solving discussions before the situation becomes job-threatening.

If a person with a disability is performing below standards, supervisors and coworkers become frustrated that the disabled employee is not contributing. If any member of a work team is incompetent or not performing to full capacity, others must take up the slack. Resentment builds, and soon that person, along with all people with disabilities, is unwelcome as a coworker and employee.

When reviewing the performance of an employee with a disability, it is especially important to focus on the outcome of the employee's work. Describe the behavior or work outcome and solicit input from the employee about how the problem can be resolved. Be prepared to accommodate the person if necessary. This does not necessarily mean to accept lower quality or quantity from the person. Most of all, do not automatically assume that performance problems are disability related.

Notes of caution:

❑ Do not try to diagnose a person's disability or second-guess the cause of the performance problem.

❑ Handle the performance problem as you would with anyone else.

Conducting Performance Appraisals

A supervisor once said, "Oh, I never do a performance appraisal on my disabled employees. It's enough that, with their disabilities, they are here and try hard. It wouldn't be fair to do a performance appraisal." Although performance appraisals may be required for all employees, how often is effort measured instead of results? If a person with a disability has the skills necessary to work, does it not make sense to evaluate the performance? Is it fair (or legal?) to deny the person feedback that could lead to improved performance and opportunities for advancement?

The answer is to conduct performance appraisals for employees with disabilities just as you would for other employees.

Generally, performance appraisals are conducted by an employee's supervisor; however, some organizations successfully combine supervisory review with peer review or self-evaluation. While appraisals generally review a person's past performance; done correctly, they can be a good counseling tool to help an employee improve and grow in the job.

Improving Work Group Relations

Most employees are helpful to each other. If employees have not worked with a person with a disability in the past, they may stumble all over themselves (and the coworker) trying to be helpful. Well-meaning but uninformed people may attempt to provide unneeded and unwanted assistance. Remind employees that the person with a disability was hired because he or she had the skills to do the job. Most people with disabilities will tell people if and when they need help.

Dog guides (now often called "service dogs") used by people with visual, hearing or mobility impairments are especially susceptible to "overhelpfulness." Employees must learn that the dog is there to work, not to play or eat. Distracting a dog guide that is in harness can be dangerous to the user, since the person depends on the dog to avoid obstacles. The employee may need to educate coworkers about relating to the dog. Once the novelty of having a dog in the workplace wears off, most people interact appropriately.

Maintaining Confidentiality

The ADA requires strict confidentiality about any employee's disability. Only supervisors and emergency personnel are permitted access to this information. People are curious, however, and will want to know "what's wrong" with the new person or present employee who becomes disabled. Reinforce that everyone is hired on the basis of ability, not disability, and that no one can answer personal questions. Most people understand when told them that personal information about them would not be released.

If an employee with a disability chooses to educate coworkers about the disability, that becomes an individual choice. However, you cannot require such personal disclosures.

Understanding Cultural Difference

No other country has a law as inclusive of people with disabilities as the United States. This is partially because other cultures have different views of people with disabilities than we do. Diversity training should include discussion of cultural perceptions of disability, and let everyone know what the ADA says about our own cultural willingness to involve persons with a disability in the mainstream of American life.

- ❏ In some cultures, a person who is born "deformed" is left to die at birth.

- ❏ In others, the person with a disability is seen as an outcast or a demon.

- ❏ In many, the family is expected to take care of the person in the home for his or her entire lifetime, and the person may never leave the home.

- ❏ In some countries, people with severe disabilities live in government-run institutions.

Promoting Inclusion

Social isolation may be a problem for an employee with a disability. Because so many people are unaccustomed to having coworkers with disabilities, they may hesitate to include them in coffee breaks, lunches, office parties, sporting events and other social events. It is important to do so, since much work information is exchanged at these times, and good working relationships are established and strengthened. To ensure greater inclusion:

- ❏ Provide training to all employees about the ADA and about the capabilities of people with disabilities.

- ❏ Introduce employees with disabilities to others in the department and encourage inclusion in lunch and coffee breaks.

Including Employees with Disabilities in Work Teams

Supervisors may be concerned about how people with disabilities will fit into quality teams, task forces or employee committees. The answer is, they will probably fit in well and use their skills to benefit the group. Having a team member with a disability will provide another perspective for problem solving and ideas for quality improvement.

Other Management Considerations

A person skilled enough to be in the workplace is skilled enough to make decisions. If job duties change or problems come up, involve the person and avoid making assumptions about needs. If outside assistance is necessary, make the disabled employee part of the team.

Total Quality Management

According to Dale Brown of the President's Committee on Employment of People with Disabilities:

> *"Quality management principals can be used throughout the process of job accommodation. The person with a disability can be treated as an internal customer. And, like all employees, when they are fully empowered to do their jobs, their productivity will grow. For companies that practice total quality management, 'accommodation' is more than a legal issue. It refers to the process of matching the communication style, work environment, expectations of the supervisor and the production system to assure that the disability of the employee does not hamper their ability to produce quality products or services."*

Handling Emergencies

Discuss emergency evacuation and safety procedures with your employees with disabilities. Ask about their experiences in previous jobs. If this is a new experience or significantly different from the past, brainstorm with your human resources, first aid or safety officer.

Examples of issues that require advance planning:

❏ Fire drills and evacuation procedures for wheelchair users, people with hearing and visual limitations, and people with developmental disabilities. If your department is on an upper floor, elevators would not be available in an emergency. Do not assume that coworkers want or should have the responsibility for carrying a wheelchair user down several flights of stairs. Liability issues may arise if either person gets hurt from improper carrying.

❏ People with developmental disabilities may need to practice emergency evacuation procedures more frequently than others. Discuss training with organizations such as the Association for Retarded Citizens or vocational rehabilitation agencies. If you have employees who are involved with an outside agency, involve the job coach in training.

Taking Disciplinary Action and Dismissal

Sometimes, it becomes necessary to terminate an employee with a disability. As with any termination, it can be painful for all involved. It is especially difficult, and potentially more questionable from a legal standpoint, if the supervisor did not communicate performance problems to the employee. If the employee is unaware of problems, being let go is even more devastating, since it happens unexpectedly.

Organizations must use the same criteria to discipline or terminate an employee with a disability as any other employee. Document poor performance, attempts at coaching and all efforts to accommodate the limitations imposed by the disability. Do not automatically assume that performance problems are caused by the disability.

If an agency such as vocational rehabilitation was involved in the hiring of the person, they may be called before taking any final action. Sometimes a third party can suggest alternatives that will solve the problem.

As with any situation like this, you will want to involve your human resources or legal department to ensure that emotions are not getting in the way of judgment and that you are following proper and legal procedures.

Preparing People with Disabilities for Promotion

The ADA covers all employment situations, not just hiring. Recognize that employees with disabilities who are serious about their careers are as interested in career development as anyone else.

Have you conducted a skills inventory of all your employees so you know who has additional skills? Do you cross-train your staff so that they are versatile in the job tasks they can perform? There are many advantages, including being able to restructure jobs to accommodate an employee with a disability.

Make sure that all your employees, including those with disabilities, receive notices of training and promotional opportunities. Encourage professional development activities such as membership in trade associations, speaking at conferences or publishing articles in professional journals.

Policies

Health Insurance

"The one issue that cuts across all lines, from the corner dry cleaner to a Fortune 500 company, is health-care costs and benefits. They'll all tell you these increases can't go on. Looking at someone's health history as a reason for hiring is less common than looking at whether or not you can insure them," according to Lisa Sprague, manager of employer benefits policy for the U.S. Chamber of Commerce.

"Discrimination is so pervasive in the workplace because of concern about health costs and absenteeism," said Gary Phelan, a Connecticut lawyer.[1]

In the last few years, employer health insurance costs have climbed dramatically, increasing an average of 10% a year between 1980 and 1986, then shooting up 15%–20% a year starting in 1987. Last year, the average U.S. company spent 26% of its net earnings—an average of $3,161 per worker—on health-care benefits.[2]

There is a perception that people with disabilities will use more health-care benefits, further driving up costs. However, many people with disabilities have stable conditions such as hearing loss, which do not require medical treatment any different from an able-bodied employee. Even when considering potential use of health benefits (which is illegal under the ADA but a common thought in employers' minds), it is important to remember that all employees have the potential for expensive accidents or illnesses.

While the law allows employers to refuse job applicants with disabilities who would pose a "significant risk" to their own or others' health and safety, issues about health and disability become intertwined. "What is the catalyst for poor health, and how is it affecting that person? It all depends on how each illness is looked at. A person may fit the definition of being disabled even if that is manifest as poor health. Employers may be on shaky legal ground by assuming that an individual's poor health makes that person a risk," according to Gary Phelan.[3]

While distinctions between health conditions and disabilities eventually will be clarified in the courts, many companies today are concerned over the need to get more information about employee health in order to contain rising insurance and workers' compensation costs.[4]

Disability Prevention

Because it is more cost-effective to prevent disabilities than to rehabilitate afterwards, organizations and their insurance companies are being proactive in this area. Statistics show that employees who return to work quickly after an injury are less likely to incur long-term disabilities.[5]

Disability prevention includes assessing a work site for potential accident or illness-causing factors and identifying and acting on conditions that may lead to extended disability once an injury occurs. "Return-to-work" programs feature treatments designed to address the injury and return the employee to the same task he or she performed prior to the injury.

Return-to-work programs cost less than traditional therapy programs and can reduce recuperation time by weeks or months. A hospital cites a $40,000 savings for each claim treated through its disability prevention program when compared to the hospital's average work injury claims. Another hospital attributes its 50% decrease in workers' compensation costs, in part, to a return-to-work program.[6]

Workers Compensation

Despite a company's best efforts at preventing accidents and injuries, there will always be some. The amount of workers' compensation funds disbursed by private carriers, public agencies and employers' self-insurance policies nationwide has been estimated at $22–$30 billion annually.

Companies should help their disabled employees return to work quickly. Light duty programs ease the way for employees to come back to work. Employers also need to work more closely with their insurance carriers to abandon the concept of disability and never-ending claim payments. It makes solid business sense to evaluate injured employees and accommodate their return to work.

Disability Management

Although there will probably always be a need for extended benefits for some injured workers, more can be done to help employees manage their disability and return to work.

About 600,000 people per year develop illness or injury that keep them off the job for at least five months. Slightly less than half return to work, which results in financial costs, reduced productivity and complications arising from strategies to absorb the loss.

Companies are becoming more aggressive in managing employee disability and its consequences. 3M and Herman Miller are often cited for their leadership focusing on early intervention, flexibility in type of job performed and a team approach involving a case manager, the supervisor, benefits representative and other relevant staff.[7]

Collective Bargaining Agreements

Approximately 24% of the U.S. manufacturing workforce is unionized,[8] and it could happen that union contracts and the ADA will conflict over accommodations for disabled members. When this happens, employers usually defer to the collective bargaining agreement and refuse to make accommodations. However, ADA regulations encourage employers and unions to avoid these conflicts by amending the contracts negotiated after the effective date of the ADA, permitting the employer to take all actions necessary to comply with the Act. Furthermore, the ADA prohibits participation in a contractual arrangement that subjects a disabled applicant or employee to discrimination.[9]

Other unaddressed issues that may cause conflict include a union's exclusive representation of all bargaining unit employees, an employer's responsibility to engage in "an informal interactive process" with employees with disabilities to arrive at an appropriate accommodation, and issues of essential job functions, seniority under collective bargaining agreements and confidentiality under the ADA.[10]

Two possible scenarios could be problematic.

- ❏ An employee may request accommodation to a position outside his or her assignment that is open but not available under terms of the collective bargaining agreement. This may be a job that would be considered "light duty" and is available based only on seniority. A person without the necessary seniority may be unable to get that job as an accommodation.

- ❏ An employee may be able to do all but one of the essential functions of a job, but the union may object to assigning that one task to a coworker to assist.

Employers who discuss possibilities with disabled individuals to determine appropriate accommodation may violate the employer's obligations under the NLRA to bargain with the representative of its employees. This possible conflict could be avoided if the union could be present during these discussions; however, such presence may conflict with the confidentiality provisions of the ADA, which requires that medical information about applicants and employees be held confidential and held in separate files.[11]

These issues could be addressed in three ways. First, collaborative long-range planning could jointly be undertaken by unions and employers. Second, a management/union committee could be established to settle ADA issues. This committee could review health and workers compensation issues, consider requests for accommodations and develop policies to determine whether reassignment or other accommodations would create an undue hardship. Third, provisions could be added to agreements negotiated after the effective date of the ADA, permitting the employer to take all actions necessary to comply. Collective bargaining agreements might include provisions under which employers agree to set aside light duty or parttime jobs that will not be filled based on seniority.

This issue requires creativity and flexibility on the part of everyone involved. In addition, all parties need to be trained on the provisions of the ADA.

What Successful Organizations Are Doing

Some companies have made the ADA work on their behalf. More than 140 corporations and labor unions have joined the Industry-Labor Council on Employment and Disability, a national, nonprofit membership organization, and employ more than 400,000 people with disabilities nationwide. Still more companies are working with other national and local organizations in developing comprehensive programs to employ and retain people with disabilities.[12] The ILC has developed a training package addressing issues such as recruiting, interviewing, testing, accommodating and integrating persons with disabilities into the work team.

What have individual companies done? Some, such as DuPont, Eastman Kodak and IBM, have developed printed materials about their experiences. National Medical Enterprises, Inc. has developed *Overcoming Challenges: A Guide to Selective Job Placement of Workers with Disabilities* and a companion resource directory for its managers. It describes implementing the company's philosophy of hiring and retaining workers with disabilities, recruiting and accommodation.

Warner-Lambert Company organized a month-long recognition of the capabilities of people with disabilities, including performances and presentations by well-known people such as violinist Itzhak Perlman, disabled by polio. Ford Motor invited psychologist and humorist Dr. Leonard Sawich to address its staff and made a video of his most informative and entertaining presentation, entitled *A Context for Understanding.* Other companies, such as Hewlett-Packard and New England Telephone, have made educational videos highlighting the accomplishments of their employees with disabilities.

Mobil and Grumman have held meetings for the EEO staff at the Human Resources Center, a vocational rehabilitation facility that provides training and placement for people with disabilities. By visiting facilities such as this, EEO staff can see how people with disabilities prepare for employment.

IBM has developed an awareness and training module, "Enabling the Disabled" for managers and employees.

Support Services for ADA Implementation

Because the ADA may present new challenges and opportunities, you may feel that there is no place to turn with questions. But answers are available, both within your organization and outside.

Support within the Organization

While supervisors will have primary responsibility for setting a tone of acceptance and working with disabled people in their area, others in the organization must set policies related to ADA compliance. Top management should be well aware of ADA compliance requirements and committed to complying. They may have developed policies, perhaps in conjunction with an attorney. The human resources department should have revised employment procedures and communicated revisions to all staff.

Many companies have set up an ADA task force, comprised of representatives throughout the organization, including perhaps an attorney, safety personnel, a human resources representative, the facilities manager and others. Progressive organizations have included present employees with disabilities to advise them on matters of policy, access and reasonable accommodation.

Honeywell Inc. has established handicapped employee councils to educate the workforce about the contributions of employees with disabilities and identify, study and make recommendations to management on issues of concern to employees with disabilities. It has developed a three-year blueprint for action on issues related to awareness, identification, hiring, career development, accommodations and accessibility.[13]

Some human resource managers have established support groups with their peers from different companies. They meet occasionally to update each other on ADA news, brainstorm ideas and solve problems. An organization might set up an internal ADA group, separate from the official ADA task force, among supervisors. Even an informal lunchtime meeting with other supervisors could be beneficial. Be sure to share success stories.

In some organizations, people with disabilities have created support groups of their own. They also have made themselves available to managers and supervisors to offer assistance in training, reviewing essential functions and assisting new employees with disabilities become successful in the organization.

Outside Support

Vocational Rehabilitation

Every state has a vocational rehabilitation agency supported by state and federal taxes. Some states have two agencies, one specializing in working with people who are blind. These agencies assist people with disabilities to become employed or maintain their employment if they become disabled. They are invaluable sources of information, as well as recruiting resources for qualified, trained people who are looking for employment. Look in the telephone directory under Vocational Rehabilitation or Commission (or Services) for the Blind in the state agencies section.

Vocational rehabilitation agencies sometimes offer job analysis and assistance in determining reasonable accommodation, especially if one of their clients is looking for a job in your area. Private rehabilitation agencies also provide training and placement support for people with disabilities.

All of the agencies should be knowledgeable about technical assistance programs and tax credits you can use to offset the possible additional costs of hiring a qualified individual with a disability.

Example: Teamwork Produces Results

A young woman worked as a waitress until she was in an automobile accident in which she sustained a traumatic brain injury leaving her with severe speech and language deficits and paralysis on the right side of her body.

She underwent extensive physical and speech therapy and rehabilitation in a traumatic brain injury program. She became a client of the vocational rehabilitation program and then took a computer training course. She was hired as a parttime file clerk in an insurance company. Because of the severity of her disabilities, she receives some assistance through the Department of Health and Welfare.

She is well accepted by the company office staff and is considered a valuable and diligent worker. She maintains an extremely motivated and enthusiastic attitude, and it is anticipated that her hours and salary will increase.

This is an example of how community organizations, medical and vocational rehabilitation, and the employer work together for success.

A man in Idaho received his GED in the Navy, worked for six years as a merchandiser for a large grocery store chain, did remodeling and painting and also worked as a maintenance worker.

He then developed severe degenerative arthritis in both wrists that required surgery. This resulted in very little use of his wrists and a 10-pound lifting restriction. He could not find a job, and he had a large family and bills and did not want to go through a long period of retraining.

Larry became a client of the Idaho Division of Vocational Rehabilitation and determined that he would like to work with computers at Idaho National Engineering Laboratory where wages and benefits would allow him to care for his family.

An occupational therapist evaluated his needs to determine if he could adapt to the computer. He needed a special chair to support his arms, a foam carpal tunnel board to support his wrists while using the keyboard, a pair of fingerless gloves to use while working at the computer, and a left wrist splint. Before beginning his work day, he must dip his wrists in heated paraffin to facilitate ease of movement.

Larry entered a Projects with Industries program, a project designed especially to provide individual training. The curriculum ranged from simple word processing to complex software and spreadsheet skills. He so impressed his instructor that he was asked to develop instructional pamphlets, on a desktop publishing program, on the use of DOS, adding special formatting, typing skills, and pictures. The manual is currently used to teach DOS in the PWI program.

Larry moved from the training program into an internship at EG&G (INEL site contractor). Since he started working, he has trained five other students. As an administrative assistant, he schedules repairs on 41 buildings, orders supplies, and checks to ensure that jobs are completed. His position calls for using the computer, good judgment, and excellent communication skills.

Community Organizations

Every community has organizations that offer services to people with disabilities and employers. Since the passage of the ADA, many have broadened their services to include employer education. Check your telephone directory under Social Service or Rehabilitation, then look for the name of a specific disability. Some agencies that serve people who are blind also have technology centers where you can view the latest equipment such as braille and speech output computers.

Supported Employment Programs

"Supported employment" refers to employing people who may be severely disabled and traditionally not in the workforce. Under supported employment, a person who is developmentally disabled, mentally ill or who has had a traumatic brain injury works with a vocational rehabilitation agency to identify skills and interests, much the same process as other clients of vocational rehabilitation agencies. An employment specialist works with an employer to identify an appropriate job for the person. Then, when the person has begun working, the job coach provided by the agency provides on-the-job training and follow-along support for the person, perhaps for several months. The job coach assures good quality and relieves the supervisor of the intense training the person may need, especially early in employment. Job coaches can also train coworkers about how to work with the employee with the disability. Generally, the role of the job coach diminishes as the person becomes more proficient and the natural support of coworkers takes over.

Example: Supported Employment

A 25-year-old man with mild mental retardation had no problem getting jobs, but was unable to maintain long-term employment because of communication problems with his supervisors.

The man became a client of a vocational rehabilitation program and was provided a job coach who helped him learn to communicate his work needs to his supervisor and learn more difficult job duties.

He is now working full time at Aluma Glass, has taken on additional duties, works overtime when needed and has increased his skill level to benefit the employer. He is now totally self-supporting, with no benefits from Social Security. He has become more socially outgoing and developed friendships and self-confidence.

While supported employment originally involved only people with developmental disabilities, companies are hiring people with other impairments. In a recent study involving supported employment for people with long-term mental illness, researchers found the following.

- Most employers who have hired workers with psychiatric disabilities found these workers had no problem integrating into the workforce

- If forced to reduce staff, more than 80% of employers said they would not automatically fire a supported-employment worker

- Eighty-four percent said they would hire another individual with mental illness

Some companies hire several employees with disabilities, usually in one area doing the same type of work, coached by one job coach who oversees and trains the group. These are called "enclaves."

Examples of supported employment include the McDonald's McJobs Program and Kentucky Fried Chicken's Project Pride. The International Association of Machinists and the Boeing Company are cooperating in a supported employment initiative where people with severe disabilities are working in both union and nonunion represented areas including wire shop and printing operations.[14]

To find out more about supported employment possibilities for your company, contact your state vocational rehabilitation agency or the county mental health or developmental disabilities agency.

High Schools

Your local high school may have a placement program for its graduates who have disabilities. You can meet with a "transition coordinator" who can identify students with skills you need in your workforce. Quite often, these students need unpaid work experience, and you may serve as a site for them. In this case, you would be under no obligation to hire, but may provide feedback about the person's skills and work habits, encouraging the person to develop further before entering the workforce fulltime.

High schools and some rehabilitation agencies sometimes have summer work experience programs for students with disabilities. If you traditionally hire extra help in the summer, consider contacting these organizations to find capable young people who need a start to their careers.

General Motors in Detroit participates in a high school partnership program, Comprehensive Leadership and Development Series (CLADS), that enables students who are physically disabled, health impaired, vision, hearing, learning or mentally disabled to take part in a two-year program of career planning and awareness and leadership development, culminating in a summer internship commensurate with the student's interests and abilities.[15]

Community Colleges and Universities

Most technical schools, colleges and universities have a Disabled Student Services Office. These offices have usually developed a strong relationship with students with disabilities throughout their academic career. They also know what accommodations have worked for them.

Recruiters can approach one of these offices, identify the jobs for which there are openings and request referrals of qualified applicants. You can also offer to serve as an internship site for a student who needs work experience. This offers your organization the opportunity to work with a student with a disability without committing to hire the person permanently. Often, students with disabilities are clients of the vocational rehabilitation system, with the support of vocational counselors and rehabilitation technology specialists who can help determine reasonable accommodations.

Citibank has entered into summer work programs with the National Technical Institute for the Deaf (NTID) in Rochester, NY. At Citibank, supervisors submit requirements to the HR department, which compiles needs and (often with supervisors) visits the campus to work with NTID staff in recruiting appropriate students for entry-level professional positions.

Supervisors undergo half-day training to gain background on deafness, and learn how to work with hearing impaired employees. Students work in such fields as data processing, work processing, accounting, industrial drafting and computer-assisted design and have benefitted in many ways, including access to the most advanced technology. The bank reports that they have gained skilled people who work hard, substitute for people on vacation and become good, long-term employees.[16]

A Successful Application of the ADA

One of the most positive steps you can take to effectively implement the ADA is to establish an on-going relationship with organizations which are knowledgeable about the capabilities of people with disabilities and work on their behalf. They will also work on your behalf to assist you in finding and successfully employing qualified individuals with disabilities.

Let's put everything together and see how you might operate in the ADA era.

Case Study #2

Chan is an accounting supervisor in a high-tech firm. The department is expanding, and he has an opening for an accounting clerk. He determines that the essential functions of the job are calculating, posting and verifying duties to obtain financial data for use in maintaining accounting records. Essential functions are:

❑ Compiling and sorting documents such as invoices and checks to substantiate business transactions

❑ Verifying and posting details of business transactions, such as funds received and disbursed, and totaling accounts

❑ Computing and recording charges, refunds, costs of damaged goods, freight charges

❑ Preparing vouchers, invoices, checks and other records using the computer

Chan determines that marginal functions of the job are keeping track of accounting office supplies and reordering when necessary and distributing accounting reports to other offices around the company.

Chan likes to give young people an opportunity and he wants someone who has had recent training in entry-level accounting work. He has heard about the ADA and would like to find a qualified person with a disability to fill the job.

If you were Chan, how would you proceed? _____

Where might you find someone with the skills you need?_____

Chan contacts the Office for Disabled Students at his local community college. He provides a copy of the job description to Flavia, the person who helps disabled students find work. Flavia knows that Kim will graduate in a few weeks with an associate's degree in accounting. She is starting to look for an entry-level job in her area and has asked Flavia to pass along job announcements to her. Flavia gives the announcement to Kim, who contacts Chan at the company. They agree to meet in Chan's office. Kim asks Chan if his office is accessible, since she is a wheelchair user. Chan assures her that the office has been assessed and should be OK.

Kim arrives at the appointed time and meets Chan. She gives him her resume, which shows good grades and some prior office work experience. Chan reviews the job description with her, asking her whether she can perform the essential functions he has outlined. She assures him she can, offering examples from her coursework and experience. Although Chan is curious about the effect her disability might have on her work, he sticks to describing the job and asking about her ability to perform essential functions.

Kim asks to see the office in which the job is located. They go into the area and discover that the partitions that make the cubicles are too close to the outside wall for her to pass. They go around another way and find that the opening of the cubicle is also too narrow for her wheelchair. They look at another office that is a little larger. They discover that the computer desk is too low for her wheelchair to fit under. Kim asks Chan how much time is spent using the computer, explaining that, because of weakness in her hands, she can be more productive using a different style keyboard.

Kim also points out to Chan that she would have difficulty performing the marginal functions listed on the job description. The accounting office supplies are in cabinets that are above her reach in the storeroom. In addition, because of the age and configuration of the building, not all offices are accessible to her, making delivery of reports difficult.

They discuss these limitations and agree that either the supplies could be moved to lower cabinets or this job duty could be assigned to someone else. In exchange, Kim could take on another duty. Also, they brainstorm ways to deliver the reports, and Chan finally admits that he has been considering offering the reports through e-mail to the other offices but has just not gotten around to setting that up.

Chan offers Kim the job, contingent upon passing the company-required drug screening and a physical exam required of all applicants to whom a job has been offered. Kim accepts, and invites Chan to the community college to see the equipment she has been using. She also invites Chan to meet her counselor from the Vocational Rehabilitation Division, who may be able to help defray expenses involved in modifying the job.

Kim passes the drug screen, and the results of the physical exam show that Kim is in good health. The doctor reviewed the job description outlining essential functions and finds no reason why Kim should not be able to perform those functions.

Chan consults the company's facility manager to request that the movable partitions be configured to allow Kim easy access to her office. The rest room, the lunchroom, the drinking fountain and other areas are accessible. He also writes up a performance expectation list and arranges for someone else to order supplies.

Chan and Kim meet with the vocational rehabilitation counselor. Chan is delighted to find that the plan for helping Kim become employed contains funding for some equipment, so costs to the company will be minimal, primarily those in making the office more accessible. The counselor also explains available tax credits to Chan, and he promises to pass the information along to the company accountant. The counselor orders the adapted computer keyboard for Kim and arranges to have it delivered to Chan's company.

At the next department meeting, Chan reviews ADA information with his work group, as well as indicating that a new employee has been hired to fill the accounting clerk position. He outlines Kim's experience and indicates that she will graduate from the community college next week. He also talks about his philosophy of hiring and supervising people with disabilities and indicates that Kim uses a wheelchair. He describes the changes that have been made in the work area to permit her wheelchair to pass unimpeded. He reminds the group that Kim was hired on the basis of her experience, her recent training, and her potential to be a productive member of the department.

He encourages his people to make her feel welcome. He assigns each member of the work group a topic for her orientation as he has done in the past for other new employees. Some members of the group ask what they have to do special for Kim, and he replies, "She is independent and capable. She may need to have something brought down from high shelves, but otherwise should need no assistance." Someone asks the cause of her disability, and Chan says, "I don't know, and her medical information is confidential, just as yours would be."

Kim's special keyboard arrives and Chan installs it. He checks to ensure that all access requirements have been completed, then walks to the door Monday morning. "Welcome, Kim. We're glad you're here."

Case Study Reveiw

Here's an example of a successful process of hiring a qualified person with a disability, involving the community college and vocational rehabilitation agency, working with the candidate to determine what modifications would maximize her potential, getting financial assistance with the costs of accommodation and resolving coworker concerns.

This is a win-win situation. You can duplicate this experience, perhaps not in the details, but in the results. What would you need to do to replicate this success?

Your New Action Plan

All the information in this book will be wasted if you do not use it—along with what you have learned about yourself—to maximize your opportunities to benefit from workers with disabilities. Let's set some goals for yourself that will help you in these efforts.

Answer the following questions thoughtfully and in as much detail as will be useful to you.

Individual Needs

Attitudinal changes I need to make: _____

_____

I need to learn more about:

The ADA _____

People with disabilities _____

Communicating effectively with those I supervise _____

How can I meet these needs?

　Training (by whom?) _____

　Talking with others in my organization (who?) _____

　Taking a class (where?) _____

　Reading (what?) _____

Things I need to discuss with my supervisor: _____

_____

The Organization Needs

Needs I have identified within the organization related to complying with the ADA and involving people with disabilities more fully in our workforce: _____

_____

Who can fill them? _____

_____

What effect can I have on seeing these needs met? _____

_____

What Can I Do?

Within my department to create an atmosphere of acceptance of people with disabilities? _____

_____

_____

To assist my staff in welcoming people with disabilities as colleagues and coworkers? _____

_____

My Goals

Regarding successfully implementing the Americans with Disabilities Act, I commit to: _____

_____

_____

Timeline to meet these identified needs:

By _____ , I will _____

_____

_____

appendix a

Resources

Job Accommodation Network

The Job Accommodation Network (JAN) is a service of the President's Committee on Employment of People with Disabilities. By calling a toll-free number (800-526-7234 or 800-ADA-WORK), you can describe to a Human Factors Consultant the limitations of a person with a disability and the type of job involved. The consultant suggests accommodations that may make it possible for the person with a disability to be successful in that job. JAN does not sell adaptive equipment, but lets you know what has worked elsewhere. In exchange, JAN would like to know your results.

Similar to JAN is the American Foundation for the Blind's Careers & Technology Information Bank, a database of more than 1,200 blind and visually impaired people who use adaptive technology at home and at work. Participants provide information about the adaptive equipment they use, their training, educational backgrounds, and professions and careers. They serve as evaluators and resource people on new adaptive technology. Employers can contact AFB at (212) 620-2080 Monday–Friday, 8:30 AM–4:30 PM, EST or write AFN, 15 West 16th Street, New York, NY 10011.

Regional Disability and Business Accommodation Centers

Each of the 10 federal regions has a Regional Disability and Business Accommodation Center set up by the National Institute on Disability and Rehabilitation Research. These offices provide free telephone assistance as well as a supply of government publications on the ADA. If the following numbers are incorrect, call (800) 949-4232 (voice or TDD) for additional information.

Region I: Connecticut, Maine, Massachusetts, New Hampshire, Rhode Island, Vermont

New England Disability and Business
Technical Assistance Center
145 Newbury St.
Portland, ME 04101
(207) 874-6535 (voice/TDD*)
(207) 874-6529 (fax)
(800) 949-4232 (voice/TDD)

Region II: New York, New Jersey, Puerto Rico, Virgin Islands

Northeast Disability and Business
Technical Assistance Center
354 South Broad St.
Trenton, NJ 08608
(609) 392-4004 (voice)
(609) 392-7004 (TDD)
(800) 487-2805 (voice)
(800) 676-2831 (TDD)

Region III: Delaware, District of Columbia, Maryland, Pennsylvania, Virginia, West Virginia

Mid-Atlantic Disability and Business
Technical Assistance Center
2111 Wilson Blvd., Suite 400
Arlington, VA 22201
(703) 525-3268 (voice/TDD)

Region IV: Alabama, Florida, Georgia, Kentucky, Mississippi, North Carolina, South Carolina, Tennessee

Southeast Disability and Business
Technical Assistance Center
1776 Peachtree Rd., Suite 310 North;
Atlanta, GA 30309
(404) 888-0022 (voice)
(404) 888-9098 (TDD)
(404) 888-9091 (fax)

Region V: Illinois, Indiana, Michigan, Minnesota, Ohio, Wisconsin

Great Lakes Disability and Business
Technical Assistance Center (M/C 627)
1640 West Roosevelt Rd.
Chicago, IL 60608
(312) 413-7756 (voice)
(312) 413-0453 (TDD)
(800) 729-8275 (voice/TDD)
(312) 413-1326 (fax)

Region VI: Arkansas, Louisiana, New Mexico, Oklahoma, Texas

Southwest Disability and Business
Technical Assistance Center
2323 S. Shepherd, Suite 1000
Houston, TX 77019
(713) 520-0232 (voice)
(713) 520-5136 (TDD)
(800) 949-4ADA (voice/TDD)

Region VII: Iowa, Kansas, Nebraska, Missouri

Great Plains Disability and Business
Technical Assistance Center
University of Missouri at Columbia
401 E. Locust St.
Columbia, MO 65201
(314) 882-3807 (voice/TDD)

Region VIII: Colorado, Montana, North Dakota, South Dakota, Utah, Wyoming

Rocky Mountain Disability and Business
Technical Assistance Center
3630 Sinton Rd., Suite 103
Colorádo Springs, CO 80907-5072
(719) 444-0252 (voice/TDD)
(800) 735-4ADA
(719) 444-0269 (fax)

Region IX: Arizona, California, Hawaii, Nevada, Pacific Basin

Pacific Disability and Business
Technical Assistance Center
440 Grand Ave., Suite 500
Oakland, CA 94610
(510) 465-7884 (voice)
(510) 465-3172 (TDD)

Region X: Alaska, Idaho, Oregon, Washington

Northwest Disability and Business
Technical Assistance Center
P.O. Box 9046,
Olympia, WA 98507-9046
(800) HELP-ADA (voice/TDD)
(206) 438-4014 (fax)

appendix b

Answers to Exercises

Match game answers (from page xv)

How well did you match up the following well-known people and their disabilities?

CONTRIBUTOR	DISABILITY
Cher	Dyslexia
Chris Burke	Down's syndrome
Bruce Jenner	Learning disability
James Brady	Head injury
Stephen Hawking	Amyotrophic lateral sclerosis
Ray Charles	Blind
Ann Jillian	Cancer
Whoopi Goldberg	Learning disability
Itzhak Perlman	Polio
Marlee Matlin	Deaf
President John F. Kennedy	Back problems
Mary Tyler Moore	Diabetes
Danny Glover	Epilepsy
Sammy Davis, Jr.	Visual impairment
Annette Funicello	Multiple sclerosis
Governor George Wallace	Paraplegia
President Franklin Roosevelt	Polio
Margaux Hemingway	Epilepsy
Virginia Woolf	Mental illness
Representative Barbara Jordan	Multiple sclerosis
Patricia Neal	Stroke

True or False Quiz Answers (from page xviii)

1. **TRUE.** The intent of ADA is to protect all "qualified individuals with disabilities." The use of "Americans" in the title is not restrictive. The ADA reflects a national sense of fairness and equality that recognizes the contributions of all individuals.

2. **TRUE.** The ADA does not invalidate or limit any federal, state or local law that provides greater or equivalent protection to individuals with disabilities. An individual may pursue a claim under all applicable laws.

3. **FALSE.** The definition of a disability is divided into three parts: a physical or mental impairment that substantially limits one or more major life activities; a record of such an impairment or being regarded as having such an impairment. Mitigating measures such as medicines or assistive or prosthetic devices do not negate the existence of an impairment.

4. **FALSE.** Economic, cultural or environmental factors such as poverty or an inadequate education are not impairments even if they are disadvantages.

5. **TRUE.** Physical characteristics that are not the result of a physiological disorder are not impairments. Similarly, personality traits that are not symptoms of a mental or psychological disorder such as poor judgment do not qualify as an impairment.

6. **FALSE.** Many impairments do not affect "major life activities." An impairment may be disabling for one individual but not for others. The "effect" of an impairment is critical and must be determined on a case-by-case consideration.

7. **FALSE.** Myths, fears and stereotypes can substantially limit a person's ability to work. Negative reactions of others cannot be used as the basis for an employment decision.

8. **FALSE.** The determination of whether an individual with a disability is qualified should be based on capabilities at the time of the employment decision. Speculation about future abilities, health conditions or possible adverse changes in insurance risks could constitute discrimination.

9. **TRUE.** One factor in determining essential functions is the number of other employees available to perform that job function. If a limited number of employees are available for the volume of work required, a function may be essential based on staff size. A similar situation might occur with a

larger work force when work flow cycles of heavy demand require intense effort followed by slow periods.

10. **FALSE.** Employers are not required to develop or maintain job descriptions. Written job descriptions, the employer's judgment, collective bargaining agreements and past employees' work experience are among the relevant evidence to be considered in determining essential job functions.

11. **FALSE.** Employers are not required to lower production standards. However, if an employer intentionally selects a level of production to exclude individuals with disabilities, the employer may have to demonstrate legitimate, nondiscriminatory reasons for that production standard.

12. **TRUE.** The ADA is intended to enable qualified individuals with disabilities to compete in the work force with or without reasonable accommodation. An accommodation is any change that enables an individual with a disability to enjoy equal employment opportunities including the application process.

13. **TRUE.** Employers are required to provide equal access to employee benefits, which may include health insurance. The ADA does not affect preexisting conditions clauses that may have an adverse affect on some employees, as long as the clauses are not used as a subterfuge to evade the purpose of the law.

14. **TRUE.** Reasonable accommodations are intended to remove or alleviate employment barriers. Reassignment to a vacant position may be reasonable if an accommodation within the individual's current position would pose an undue hardship. The reassignment may not be used to limit, segregate or otherwise discriminate. It should be an equivalent position. Reassignment is not available to new applicants.

15. **FALSE.** Accommodations include areas that must be accessible for work as well as nonwork areas used by all employees. Lunch rooms, training areas and restrooms may be subject to modifications to achieve reasonable accommodations.

16. **FALSE.** Rescheduling a job by altering when an essential function is performed may be a reasonable accommodation when a disability precludes performance at a customary hour.

17. **TRUE.** Any significant expense or difficulty that would fundamentally alter the operation of a business may be an "undue hardship." However, if an alternative accommodation would not create an undue hardship, the employer would be required to provide that reasonable accommodation.

18. **TRUE.** An employer may refuse to hire an otherwise qualified individual with a disability who poses a direct threat to himself or others if no accommodation exists that would eliminate or reduce the risk. An employer may not deny employment based on a slightly increased risk. All considerations must be made on a case-by-case basis.

19. **FALSE.** Drug testing is not considered a medical examination. The ADA neither encourages nor prohibits testing for illegal use of drugs.

20. **FALSE.** It is unlawful to discriminate against any qualified individual because that person is known to have an association with an individual who is disabled. This protection is not limited to a familial relationship.

21. **FALSE.** Any accommodation is sufficient as long as it meets the job-related needs of the individual. The employer should consider all factors, including employee preference, effectiveness and cost when making a decision.

22. **FALSE.** An employer cannot be expected to accommodate a disability when there is no knowledge of its existence. It is the responsibility of the individual with a disability to request an accommodation if needed.

23. **FALSE.** The ADA is not an affirmative action program. It does not require preferences favoring individuals with disabilities over other applicants. The ADA requires employers to remove employment barriers to ensure equal employment opportunities.

24. **TRUE.** If an accommodation is necessary, and refused, the individual may not be able to perform the essential functions of the job and would no longer be qualified.

25. **FALSE.** Medical examinations and inquiries as to the nature or severity of a disability are prohibited before a job offer is made. However, an employer may ask applicants to demonstrate how they would perform job-related functions with or without a reasonable accommodation.

26. **TRUE.** Job-related dexterity tests may be given to all similarly situated applicants at any point in the application or employment process, consistent with business necessity and with reasonable accommodation if requested. Such tests are not considered medical examinations.

27. **TRUE.** A job-related medical examination may be required after making an offer of employment. Employment may be based on the results of the examination, provided all entering employees in the same job category are subject to such an examination.

28. **FALSE.** Medical examinations may be required to determine fitness for duty. The collection of this information should be on separate forms and treated as confidential medical records.

29. **TRUE.** The individual with a disability could volunteer to pay for a part or all of the cost of an accommodation found to be an undue hardship. Alternative sources of funding such as a qualified tax credit or a grant might also be used to reduce cost to an acceptable level.

30. **TRUE.** The spirit of ADA is intended to provide individuals with disabilities access to the mainstream of American life. While legal remedies are available, common sense and constructive attitudes will result in substantial benefits to all parties.

endnotes

Introduction

1. Brochure from JAN: A Service of the President's Committee on Employment of People with Disabilities (1-800-526-7234), p. 5.

2. Brochure from JAN: A Service of the President's Committee on Employment of People with Disabilities (1-800-526-7234), p. 5.

Part One

1. Technical Assistance Manual of the ADA

2. ADA Technical Assistance Manual

3. ADA Technical Assistance Manual

4. ADA Technical Assistance Manual

5. ADA Technical Assistance Manual

6. ADA Technical Assistance Manual

Part Two

1. Witt, Melanie Astaire. *Job Strategies for People with Disabilities: Enable Yourself for Today's Job Market.* Princeton, NJ: Peterson's Guides, 1992, p. 103.

2. The section on Disability Awareness Training is adapted from Dickson, Mary B. and Michael Mobley, *The Americans with Disabilities Act: Impact on Training.* Alexandria, VA: American Society for Training and Development, March 1992.

3. Mathews, Jay. "Disabilities Act Prompts More People to Come Forward," in *The Houston Chronicle,* Nov. 27, 1992, Business, p. 4.

Part Three

1. From "An Employer's Guide to the Americans with Disabilities Act" by Abell and Cane, p. 15-4.

2. From "An Employer's Guide to the Americans with Disabilities Act" by Abell and Cane, p. 15-4.

3. From "An Employer's Guide to the Americans with Disabilities Act" by Abell and Cane, p. 15-4.

4. Hine, MD, Matthew M., "Keeping Medical Evaluations in Tune with the ADA," in *Reasonable Accommodation: The Journal of Disability Management and ADA Compliance,* vol. 1, no. 2, July/August 1993.

5. Op. cit., pp. 10–11.

6. Ibid.

7. Berry, Mark W., "Drug Testing and the ADA," in *Employment Law Advisory Bulletin.* Bellevue, WA: Davis Wright Tremaine, Spring 1993.

8. Quoted from "An Employer's Guide to the Americans with Disabilities Act" by Abell and Cane, pp. 15-3 and 15-4.

Part Four

1. Brochure from JAN: A Service of the President's Committee on Employment of People with Disabilities (1-800-526-7234), p. 5.

2. Brochure from JAN: A Service of the President's Committee on Employment of People with Disabilities (1-800-526-7234), p. 5.

3. Adapted from Annett, Mark. "A Guide for Making Reasonable Accommodation," in *Reasonable Accommodation: The Journal of Disability Management and ADA Compliance,* vol. 1, no. 2, July/August 1993, pp. 6–9.

4. From "An Employer's Guide to the Americans with Disabilities Act" by Abell and Cane, p. 15-9–15-10.

5. From "An Employer's Guide to the Americans with Disabilities Act" by Abell and Cane, p. 15-8–15-9.

6. Vol. 2, No. 6, June 1993, p. 38.

7. From "An Employer's Guide to the Americans with Disabilities Act" by Abell and Cane, p. 15-8–15-9.

8. From "An Employer's Guide to the Americans with Disabilities Act" by Abell and Cane, p. 15-8–15-9.

9. From "An Employer's Guide to the Americans with Disabilities Act" by Abell and Cane, p. 15-10.

Part Five

1. O'Brien, Timothy L., "Disabled Get New Weapons in Battle Against Discrimination; New federal, state legislation takes aim at bias in workplace," in *Newsday*, Sept. 1, 1991, p. 106.

2. Ibid.

3. Ibid.

4. Ibid.

5. Smith, Gregory T., "Guest Commentaries: Disability prevention pays off," in *Oregon Health Forum*, Vol. 3, No. 7, July 1993, p. 11.

6. Ibid.

7. Smart, op. cit., p. 72.

8. Grant Thornton. *Grant Thornton Manufacturing Climate Student.* Chicago, IL: Author, in collaboration with Prentice Hall, 1990.

9. Bruyere, Susanne M., "The Implication of the ADA for Labor Relations, Collective Bargaining, and Contract Administration," in *Journal of Rehabilitation Administration* Special Issue—Americans with Disabilities Act and Employment: Does it Work?, vol. 17, no. 3, p. 123, August 1993.

10. Ibid.

11. Ibid.

12. Smart, Lana. "Improving Employment Opportunities for Persons with Disabilities: A Thumbnail Sketch of Corporate Initiatives," in *Employment and Disability: Trends and Issues for the 1990s.* Alexandria, VA: National Rehabilitation Association, 1990, p. 71.

13. Smart, op. cit., p. 72.

14. Smart, op. cit., p. 72.

15. Smart, op. cit., p. 72.

16. Smart, op. cit., p. 72.

BIBLIOGRAPHY

Aalberts, R. J., and D. W. Hardigree. "Risk Management and Insurance Implications Associated with the Americans with Disabilities Act: Accessibility to Places of Public Accommodation," *Journal of Insurance Issues,* 15(2), 1, 1992.

Americans with Disabilities Act Technical Assistance Manual. Prepared jointly by the Equal Employment Opportunity Commission and the Justice Department. Available from the closest U.S. Government Printing Office Bookstore.

Atlas, R. "Will ADA Handicap Security? How Will the Americans with Disabilities Act (ADA) Affect Security?" *Security Management,* 36(3), 37, 1992.

Bolles, Richard Nelson. *Job-Hunting Tips for the So-Called Handicapped or People Who Have Disabilities.* Berkeley, CA: Ten Speed Press, 1991.

Brislin, J. A. "The Effects of the Americans with Disabilities Act Upon Medical Insurance and Employee Benefits," *Employee Benefits Journal,* 17(1), 9, 1992.

Dickson, Mary B. *Supervising Employees with Disabilities: Beyond ADA Compliance.* Menlo Park, CA: Crisp Publications, Inc., 1993.

Dickson, Mary B. and Michael Mobley. *The Americans with Disabilities Act: Impact on Training.* Alexandria, VA: American Society for Training and Development, 1992.

Dickson, Mary, B. and Michael Mobley. *The Americans with Disabilities Act: Techniques for Accommodation.* Alexandria, VA: American Society for Training and Development, 1992.

DuPont Company. *Equal to the Task II: 1990 DuPont Survey of Employment of People with Disabilities.* Write DuPont, Attn: G51932, P.O. Box 90029, Wilmington, DE 19880-0029, or call (800) 527-2601.

Feldblum, C. "Medical Examinations and Inquiries Under the Americans with Disabilities Act: A View from the Inside," *Temple Law Review,* 64(2), 521.

Fitzpatrick, R. B., and E. A. Benaroya. "Americans with Disabilities Act and AIDS," *The Labor Lawyer,* 8(2), 249, 1992.

Frierson, James G. *Employer's Guide to The Americans with Disabilities Act.* Washington, D.C.: BNA Books, 1992.

Fritz, G. and N. Smith. *The Hearing Impaired Employee: An Untapped Resource.* San Diego: College-Hill Press, 1985.

Gordon, P. L. "The Job Application Process after the Americans with Disabilities Act," *Employee Relations Law Journal,* 18(2), 185, 1992.

Jamieson, David and Julie O'Mara. *Managing Workforce 2000: Gaining the Diversity Advantage.* San Francisco: Jossey-Bass Publishers, 1991.

Koen Jr., C. M., S. J. Hartman, and S. M. Crow. "Health Insurance: The ADA's Missing Link," *Personal Journal,* 70(11), 82, 1991.

Koglin, Oz Hopkins. "Looking into Hell: Progress in Brain Research Gives Insight into the Biology of Mental Disorders," *The Oregonian.* Dec. 31, 1992.

Kohl, J. P., and P. S. Greenlaw. "The Americans with Disabilities Act of 1990: Implications for Managers," *Sloan Management Review,* 33(3), 87, 1992.

Koslow, S., and M. White. "Employer-Sponsored Health Benefits Under the ADA," *Mental and Physical Disability Law Reporter,* 16(5), 560, 1992.

In the Mainstream. Mainstream Inc., 3 Bethesda Metro Center, Suite #830, Bethesda, MD 20814. (301) 654-2400 (v/tdd), (301) 654-2403 (fax). Bimonthly newsletter, $20 per year. Mainstream also has an information packet of 11 articles on the accommodation process with examples of successful accommodations for $20.

Mancuso, L. L. "Reasonable Accommodations for Workers with Psychiatric Disabilities," *Psychosocial Rehabilitation Journal,* 14, 3–19, 1990.

McAdams, T., F. Moussavi, and M. Klassen. "Employee Appearance and the Americans with Disabilities Act: An Emerging Issue?" *Employee Responsibilities and Rights Journal,* 5(4), 323, 1992.

New Horizons: A Guide for Supervisors Working with the Handicapped (pamphlet for Jersey Bell employees, but includes general information as well), 1984.

New York Telephone. *Supervisor Responsibilities Toward Handicapped Individuals, Special Disabled Veterans and Vietnam Veterans* (pamphlet for New York Telephone employees, but includes general information as well), 1983.

Pimentel, Richard K., et al. *The Workers' Compensation-ADA Connection: Supervisory Tools for Workers' Compensation Cost Containment That Reduce ADA Liability.* Chatsworth, CA: Milt Wright & Associates, Inc., 1993.

President's Committee on Employment of People with Disabilities. *Ready, Willing, and Available: A Business Guide for Hiring People with Disabilities.* Revised August 1992. (202) 376-6200 (voice), (202) 376-6205 (TDD), (202) 376-6219 (fax). The President's Committee also has pamphlets on working with people with specific disabilities.

Public Attitudes Toward People with Disabilities. Available for $25 from National Organization on Disability, 910 16th Street NW, Suite 600, Washington, DC 20006.

Risk Watch, a newsletter published by the Public Risk Management Association (PRIMI). Available from PRIMI, 1117 N. 19th St., Suite 900, Arlington, VA 22209, (703) 528-7701. Updates members on federal legislation and regulations that may affect risk management policies and procedure.

Segal, Jonathan A., "Drugs, Alcohol and the ADA," in *HR Magazine,* Dec. 1992, pp. 73–76.

U.S. Department of Labor. *An Employer's Guide to Dealing with Substance Abuse,* 1990. Brochure available from the National Clearinghouse for Alcohol and Drug Information, P.O. Box 2345, Rockville, MD 20847, (301) 468-2600 or (800) 729-6686.

Witt, Melanie Astaire. *Job Strategies for People with Disabilities.* Princeton, NJ: Peterson's Guides, 1992.

ABOUT THE AUTHOR

Mary B. Dickson is president of Creative Compliance Management, a consulting firm which assists organizations in maximizing their human resources. She hepls them confidently and cost-effectively implement the Americans with Disabilities Act. She provides training and consultation in all aspects of ADA implementation and issues related to employees with disabilities.

❑ ADA policy development

❑ job analysis and job descriptions

❑ awareness, sensitivity, and communication to coworkers and customers with disabilities

❑ supervisory concerns

❑ assistance with individual employee situations

Ms. Dickson serves as a technical consultant to media firms developing ADA training materials. In addition, she conducts training on a variety of management and supervisory development topics.

She is the author of *Supervising Employees with Disabilities: Beyond ADA Compliance,* published in 1993 by Crisp Publications, Inc., and is co-author of *The Americans with Disabilities Act: Impact on Training* and *The Americans with Disabilities Act: Techniques for Accommodation* published by the American Society for Training and Development (ASTD) in 1992. She is Past National Director of ASTD's Disabilities Awareness Network.

Ms. Dickson has a master's degree in vocational rehabilitation from the University of Wisconsin-Stout. She is a former Director of Rehabilitation Services for the Oregon Commission for the Blind and taught at the Center for Continuing Education in Rehabilitation at Seattle University. She has hired and supervised people with disabilities.

Ms. Dickson welcomes your comments and questions. She also welcomes the opportunity to talk with you about how her training and consulting services could benefit your organization. You may reach her at:

Creative Compliance Management
13629 SE Grant Court
Portland, OR 97233
(503) 255-9318   (503) 255-7408 (fax)   email consltant@aol.com

NOTES

NOTES

NOTES

NOTES